The Best of EFY

The Best of EFY

DESERET
BOOK

SALT LAKE CITY, UTAH

Library of Congress Cataloging-in-Publication Data

The best of EFY : favorite talks from more than a decade of Especially for Youth programs.
    p.   cm.
    ISBN 1-59038-097-5 (pbk.)
    1. Mormon youth—Religious life. 2. Mormon youth—Conduct of life. 3. Church of Jesus Christ of Latter-day Saints—Doctrines. 4. Especially for Youth (Program) I. Especially for Youth (Program) II. Title.
BX8643.Y6B475 2003
248.8'3'088283—dc21   2003004431

Printed in the United States of America   7973-7114
Bang Printing, Brainerd, MN

10 9 8 7 6 5 4 3 2 1

CONTENTS

Contents

1

"COME UNTO ME"

R. Scott Simmons

I love teaching seminary. However, one challenging aspect of the job is helping students to "experience" the scriptures. One day, while preparing a lesson on Matthew 11:28–30, I was having just such a challenge. I wanted my students to do more than read the passage. I wanted them to truly experience what the Savior meant when he said, "Come unto me." Then inspiration struck. I quickly gathered objects I would need for the lesson and headed to class.

Following the devotional, I walked to the front of the room and placed a chair so that it was facing the class. I noticed that my class members were almost as nervous as I was. (I'm known for my—sometimes—interesting teaching techniques.) The class waited in silence as I carefully dusted off the chair. Then, without warning, I said, "Matt, come up here." At that point the class relaxed. Now, Matt was the only one who needed to worry. Slowly, he made his way to the front. Casually, I asked him to sit down. After carefully checking the chair for anything out of the ordinary, he did. I then asked Matt to take off his shoes and socks. Three girls sitting off to the right screamed, "No!!!" You see, Matt was a basketball player, and I guess, strange as it may seem, they had somehow smelled Matt's feet before. However, at that point, Matt began to relax and enjoy the situation. He took each shoe off with the flair of a performer, much to the aversion of the three girls.

When he had finished taking off his shoes, I reminded him, "Matt, the socks, too." Again the girls screamed. So Matt did what any true senior boy in that situation would do: he threw one of his socks at the lead girl. It wouldn't have been that big of a deal, except this young lady had what I call "bangs to heaven." Her bangs went straight up for a good five inches. This effect is achieved by sculpting them into place with massive amounts of hair spray while riding a motor scooter at a high rate of speed. Because of the combination of hair spray and the height of her bangs, the sock stuck.

After finally getting the class under control and convincing the young lady who had been hit by the sock that she wasn't melting (the result of watching the *Wizard of Oz* too many times), I turned my attention back to Matt. I interrupted his enjoyment of his sock toss by pulling out a blindfold. The class once again focused on the situation at hand.

At this point I blindfolded Matt, spun him around ten times, and asked him to find his way to the back of the room. The class was silent as Matt teetered his way to the chalkboard. Once he found the chalkboard, he oriented himself and headed toward the back of the room. At that point everything got exciting.

My first period students were all kind, loving, and charitable. NOT! They did everything in their power to keep Matt from reaching the back of the room. Students started sliding desks toward him. They rearranged the furniture. Two boys got the piano and began moving it back and forth in front of him. (Matt must have thought this was the longest piano he had ever felt.) Finally, Matt got fed up. He climbed over the piano as well as three students and made it to the back of the room. As he went to take his blindfold off, I stopped him and said, "Matt, before you take off your blindfold I want to ask you a few questions. First of all, what was it like trying to find the back of the room, blindfolded?" He said it was hard.

"Why?" I asked.

He replied, "Because this class is a bunch of jerks."

"Okay, other than that, why was it hard?"

"Well, mostly because I couldn't see."

I said, "Matt, you made it to the back of the room. Do you think you could now make it back to the front of the room?"

"No problem, Brother Simmons. This time I know what to watch out for and which direction to go."

"Okay, Matt. Find the front of the room." As Matt went to step forward, I stopped him.

"Wait just a minute." While Matt paused, I reached in my coat pocket, pulled out a huge box of thumbtacks, and shook them for all to hear. In unison, the whole class took a deep breath. With my class not breathing, I scattered the tacks all over the floor in front of Matt. Everyone leaned forward in their seats as I said, "Matt, go ahead." Now, I had picked Matt on purpose. He had big feet. That meant more tacks per foot. He didn't move. I repeated, "Matt, go ahead."

He slowly backed up so that he was flat against the door and said, "Nope. No way. I'm not movin'."

I said, "Matt, what's the matter? Why not?" (Teachers sometimes ask dumb questions to make a point.)

Matt simply replied, "There are tacks all over the floor." The class sat motionless. I wondered if they were still breathing. I hadn't heard them breathe out since sucking all the oxygen out of the room.

With the tension mounting, I said, "Matt, you're blindfolded. You can't see. How do you know there are tacks on the floor?"

He said, "I heard you shake the box, I heard the tacks hit the floor, and I heard the class suck all the oxygen out of the room. I'm not movin'." Wanting my class to breathe again, I said, "Okay, I'll tell you what. You pick someone in the room you trust."

It was interesting to watch the class as Matt began to contemplate who he would pick. His friends began to point to themselves, gesturing like, "He's going to pick me."

Finally, after several seconds, he said, "I want Amy." I realize that doesn't mean much to the reader because you don't know Amy.

Amy was the most quiet girl in the class. I was honestly surprised that he even knew her name. She was not someone Matt would date or even hang out with, but he trusted her. Why? Because Amy was good. She was righteous. Matt knew it. Everyone knew it. You should have seen the shocked look on Matt's friend's faces when he chose Amy. (Isn't it sad that more people in tough situations don't put their trust in someone righteous?)

I said, "Amy, please come here." Amy made her way slowly to the back of the class. I then asked Amy to lead Matt through the tacks. I placed no restrictions on how she did it. I simply told her to lead him through the tacks. That's what makes this object lesson interesting. I've staged this demonstration a hundred times since, and I've probably seen a hundred ways to lead people through the tacks. Some people simply sweep the tacks out of the way. Others try to talk them through. One young man pulled a magnet out of his pocket and picked up all the tacks with it. (I still haven't figured out what he was doing with a magnet that big in his pocket.) My favorite experience came when one rather muscular girl grabbed the poor boy that was blindfolded and carried him bodily through the maze of tacks.

In the many times I've used this object lesson, only once have I seen what I'm about to tell you. Again, I said, "Amy, lead Matt through the tacks." As we all waited and watched to see what Amy would do, Matt caught us off guard. He reached out. He extended his hand toward Amy. Matt is the only student that ever reached out. Everyone else has just stood there waiting for the person to come to them. Matt reached out.

Recently, I've been amazed at how many of my students are in the same situation Matt was. They are figuratively up against a wall, afraid to move because of the tacks they fear. The only difference is their tacks are spiritual instead of physical. In every case, the real problem is not the tacks or even the blindfold. The problem is they are unwilling to reach out. They are waiting for someone to come and get them, rather than reaching out to someone they can trust.

When the Savior said, "Come unto me," he was inviting us to reach out and trust him (see 2 Nephi 26:23–24). Are there tacks in your life? Are you up against a wall, spiritually, and afraid to move for fear of getting hurt? Reach out. The Savior is ever ready to lead you through your tacks if you just trust and reach out (see D&C 78:18). The real question is, how do we reach out? Let me share with you three ways.

Prayer

First, pray. Pray morning and night. Pray during the day. Pray always in your heart. Pray. In one scripture passage alone (3 Nephi 18:15–23) the Savior mentions prayer eight times. Now when I say pray, I mean *really* pray. Not the old "Now I lay me down to sleep . . ." prayer. Let me illustrate.

The other day I asked my students to show me how they pray. I was amazed at what I saw. Some were lying on the floor. Others were draped over their desks, like they do to their bed. One young man remarked, "I always pray while lying in my bed. That way, if I fall asleep during my prayer, when I wake up in the morning I just have to say amen. Then I count that as my morning prayer, too." As I said, I was amazed. Try something: the next time you say your prayers, kneel in the middle of your room where you can't lean on anything. Some of you may have to clear a spot, but do it (see Enos 1:4). I promise you, if you will do this thing, it will make a difference in your prayers.

Once you're kneeling, and not leaning or lying down, talk to your Father in Heaven out loud (see D&C 19:28). Tell him what's in your heart and on your mind (see Alma 34:27). Tell him what your tacks are and how you feel about them. Be open and honest. Some of you may be thinking that there are some things you could never tell your Father in Heaven. I have news for you: he already knows. So why doesn't he just help you? He loves you enough not to infringe on your agency. Because of this sacred gift of agency, you and I need to reach out—to him. We can tell him everything.

When you finish your prayer, don't jump up and rush into your day or into your bed. Pause a minute. You may not get an answer, but you will know your Father has heard your prayer (see Philippians 4:6–7). You will find the promise found in Doctrine and Covenants 88:63 is true. "Draw near unto me and I will draw near unto you; seek me diligently and ye shall find me; ask, and ye shall receive; knock, and it shall be opened unto you."

Scripture Study

Second, study your scriptures. Someone once wisely said, "If you want to talk to God, pray. If you want God to talk to you, read your scriptures." The scriptures are the words of Christ. When likened (1 Nephi 19:23) to ourselves, they will "tell you all things what ye should do" (2 Nephi 32:3).

One major roadblock to studying the scriptures comes from the idea that we always need to start at the beginning. Perhaps this is the reason so many members of the Church have 1 Nephi 1:1 memorized. "I, Nephi, having been born . . ." I'll bet you finished the sentence, didn't you? Instead of always starting at the beginning, try opening the book to wherever it opens, or look up specific topics in the Topical Guide. As you read, think about your tacks. Ask yourself, "How can what I'm reading help me through my tacks?" Ponder what you need or what you have read. As you do, the scriptures will come alive.

Young people often share experiences with me of how the scriptures have answered their prayers. For example, one young lady told me she had really been trying to live the gospel. Yet she still felt spiritually empty. One day she opened her scriptures to Alma 34 and read verses 17–27, which are about praying. As she read, she thought, *I'm doing all that, so why do I feel so spiritually empty?* Then she read the next verse: "Do not suppose that this is all; for after ye have done all these things, if ye turn away the needy, and the naked, and visit not the sick and afflicted, and impart of your substance [to the poor] . . . your prayer is vain" (verse 28). The scriptures came alive! She realized she had been forgetting the second great commandment, to love others (see Matthew 22:39). She wasn't serving others! The next day she volunteered to feed the homeless. As she served, she found the spirituality she had been missing. She walked through the tacks unharmed because she reached out.

Service

Third, serve other people. In Matthew 11:29 the Savior invites us to take his yoke upon us. What does that mean? A yoke is used to attach two animals together for the purpose of increasing the amount they can carry or pull. Notice that the Savior doesn't say, "Let me take your yoke." Rather, he tells us to take his yoke. He's inviting us to join him in his work. And what is his work? "To bring to pass the immortality and eternal life of man" (Moses 1:39). He desires to help our brothers and sisters make it home. So how do we help the Savior? We do so by serving other people. We must look for opportunities to help others. In my seminary classes, I assign two people to be what I call "secret service agents." Their assignment is to secretly do nice things for members of the class. It is amazing what this will do for the morale and spirituality of a class, not to mention what it does for the people who perform the service.

Each morning I make it a point to kneel down and ask Heavenly Father who I can help that day. Each day, he tells me. (You know, it's funny, but I've never asked who I could help and had him say, "Thanks for the offer, but we've got it covered.") There is always someone who needs help.

One day while working at the seminary, I got a strong impression to telephone a close friend. I stopped what I was doing and made the call. We talked for over an hour. It seems he was really having a hard time making some difficult decisions and just needed someone to talk to. As we concluded our conversation, he thanked me, and then almost as an afterthought, added, "You must have been inspired." I had no sooner hung up the phone when I felt impressed to call my mom and tell her I loved her. I know it sounds like I watch too many of those Mormon commercials, but I called. We visited for a minute, and then I simply said, "Mom, I just called to say I love you."

Mom asked, "How did you know?"

I said, "Know what?" She told me it had been a hard day and that she really needed someone to let her know she was loved. Sometimes service can be as simple as a phone call. Don't always wait to be prompted. Remember to be "anxiously engaged in a good cause, and do many things of [your] own free will" (D&C 58:27).

Reach out. Pray. Study your scriptures. Serve. As you do so, the Savior will "lead [you] by the hand" through your personal maze of tacks and "give [you] answer[s] to [your] prayers" (D&C 112:10).

R. Scott Simmons served a mission to Cleveland, Ohio, then attended Brigham Young University and worked at the Missionary Training Center. He has taught seminary and has been an instructor in the Department of Church History and Doctrine at BYU. Currently he is CES coordinator in Austin, Texas. Scott married Nancy Wright in the Jordan River Utah Temple in 1992. They are the proud parents of a little boy named Matthew. Scott's favorite things to do include teaching, studying Church history, going on outdoor adventures, and spending time with his wife and son.

2

FOLLOWING THE SAVIOR'S EXAMPLE

Mary Ellen Edmunds

Can you remember an experience in your life when you actually stopped and consciously asked yourself, "What would Jesus do?" If you can, you might feel the same way I do: That the question, and the answer, and what you did, made a huge difference in the experience and even in your life.

On a Saturday a while ago, I was returning home from a trip to California. My car had been at the Salt Lake airport for a few days, and it was pretty dirty. I was in a hurry (no surprise there), but I decided to stop in Springville and get the car washed. I pulled in with my car-wash token ready to pop in the slot. I wasn't going to waste a motion or a minute! But there was a "boat car" ahead of me, and it wasn't going anywhere. I found myself getting annoyed. "What's going on? Why isn't he moving?"

Then I noticed the driver leaning out the window, putting a bill in the machine, and then watching as it came back out. He kept trying. He kept getting it back. I counted about seven times. At first I was so frustrated. All kinds of conversations went on in my head in just a few seconds about what I'd like to say to him. But for some reason, I started watching myself rather than him. I began to be aware of how unfair it was for me to be upset with him rather than trying to understand what was happening and perhaps help. Slowly but surely (thank goodness), I changed my attitude from annoyance to wanting to figure out what was happening. This was an interesting experience for me.

I'm always saying in talks that we should be more Christlike—that we should seriously ask ourselves, "What would Jesus do" and then try to do it. So I was sitting there in my car thinking things like, "Are you going to do the right thing? Are you going to do what you recommend others should do? Will you think hard about what Jesus would do and then do it?" It made me feel good that I accomplished a change in my feelings about this man and having to wait for him. Instead of being annoyed, I wanted to help. I really wanted to help. So I got out of the car and walked up to the "boat car." The driver was an older guy. He was puzzled; he just couldn't figure out how to get the thing to work. He was holding a one-dollar bill. He said the machine wouldn't take it. I said, "I wonder if it'll take a token." He seemed a bit puzzled. "Oh . . . well, maybe." I think he was con-fused, knowing he didn't have one of those. Then I showed him mine. There it was, in my hand, the token I'd had ready so I could wash my car. It didn't have my name on it or anything. I didn't remember ever having to punch in my social security number or birth date or home phone number or the score of the last Super Bowl game when I used one of those car-wash tokens. Maybe it would work as well for a "boat" as it did for my own car. But he still wasn't comprehending that I wanted to help him—to give him a gift. I just said something like, "Well, let's try it and see what happens." I'm not sure that's exactly what Jesus would have said, but in my heart it felt pretty close. "Okay!" he said, as if we were going to participate together in a great experiment, a new adventure.

So I pushed the button for a wash and then put my token in, and the green light came on ("Pull Forward"). "It worked!" I hollered with genuine enthusiasm. "There you go!" He was so excited! He kept say-ing thanks as he was pulling forward. I don't think he even realized that I'd given him the token. He was still holding his one-dollar bill. I wasn't concerned about money—I was just hoping he'd get his window rolled up before the water and soap started shooting all over the place. I got in my car and watched to make sure he was going in far enough and that the "boat" wash was underway, and then I just drove off . . . feeling very, very good inside.

I wish I could be that way *all* the time—kind and willing and ready to help others. But so often—too often—my initial response is very much "natural man," being annoyed and frustrated and all. I feel like a hypocrite when that happens, because I say all these flowery words to others about doing good and being good. It seems to me that there is a lot of pure joy in honestly trying to figure out what Jesus would do and then doing it. It might be even sweeter when it's a situation where someone is not going to be able to pay you back. They might not even know who you are. And if they ask, you could always say, "Oh, I'm just an instrument" or something like that to throw them off the trail.

President Howard W. Hunter said: "Let us follow the Son of God in all ways and in all walks of life. Let us make him our exemplar and our guide. We should at every opportunity ask ourselves, 'What would Jesus do?' and then be more courageous to act upon the answer. We must follow Christ, in the best sense of that word. We must be about his work as he was about his Father's. We should try to be like him, even as the Primary children sing, 'Try, try, try'" (*Ensign,* November 1994, 87).

That's good, isn't it? It sounds like President Hunter knew that it often takes courage to act upon the feelings that come into our hearts when we're wondering what Jesus would do. Can you think of any examples from your own life, as you're reading along? Often I learn a lot when I look back at my experiences and talk to myself (or someone I trust) about how different a situation could have been if I'd only asked the question and acted upon the answer. For example, what kind of a driver would Jesus be? How would he respond to other drivers on the roads and freeways? When I sincerely ask myself that question, I find that I'm probably not doing what Jesus would do often enough. I don't think he'd call other drivers names and get frustrated when they got in his way. I'm working to ask myself much more often as I drive, "What would Jesus do?"

Another example might be in asking myself how Jesus would treat friends, neighbors, and even family members. When I was younger and living at home, I sometimes found myself "justifying" what I said or did by thinking that even Jesus would have punched my brother for what he did! There are powerful accounts in the scriptures of the way Jesus did treat others. He was very unselfish and kind. He always seemed to think of others first. He took time; he wasn't in such a big hurry as I so often am. He didn't seem annoyed when people followed him around, even when he may have been seeking a chance to be alone to talk to his Father or rest.

Have you ever had a time when someone said something unkind about you that wasn't true? Or did something to you that wasn't fair? Have you ever felt like you wanted to "get even"? I can tell you from my own experience that trying to figure out what Jesus would do, even in a situation like this where you know what's been said isn't true, or what was done wasn't right, you'll probably end up being nice rather than finding a way to "get even." And you'll feel okay about it! Amazing! There are times when rather than asking, "What would Jesus do?" it might be easier to ask, "What would Jesus want me to do right now?" For me, that usually works as well as wondering what he would do. He would always want me to do the right thing, the kind thing, the thing which would leave me with peace of mind rather than guilt at having been unkind or unthoughtful or unfair. I've noticed people wearing bracelets and rings and things that have "WWJD" carved on them. Maybe our CTR ring will help us in the same way. Or maybe we can just keep the question in our minds and in our hearts and let it become a good habit. Several years ago, I read a book called *In His Steps* by Charles Sheldon. He told the story of a group of people who went to the same church. They promised each other that for a whole year they would honestly try to do what Jesus would do—that they would ask themselves that question in every aspect of their lives and act upon their answer, no matter what. Could I do that? Could we? It's incredible to read the account of how lives changed—not just the lives of those who made and kept that promise, but of those who noticed. And that reminds me of one of the best things about trying to do what Jesus would do. It is described in part of a hymn: "Example sheds a genial ray of light which men are apt to borrow" ("Let Each Man Learn to Know Himself," *Hymns,* 1948, no. 91). Somewhere there might be an old man in a nice, clean "boat car" looking around for someone who needs a car-wash token.

Mary Ellen Edmunds describes herself as a woman who wants to do good and be good. A former director of training at the Missionary Training Center in Provo, Utah, she was also a member of the general board of the Relief Society of The Church of Jesus Christ of Latter-day Saints. She is a graduate of the College of Nursing at Brigham Young University and has served full-time proselyting and welfare missions in Asia and Africa.

3

WHAT ARE YOU CARRYING IN YOUR BACKPACK?

John Bytheway

Back when I was a new Boy Scout, our teachers quorum had planned an overnight backpacking trip. The plan was to show up at our Scoutmaster's house at 7:00 AM on Friday, but you know how it is, somebody's always late. Somebody's alarm didn't go off, someone else forgot his mess kit, or we'd have to stop and put gas in the car. We finally left at about 1:30 in the afternoon. Good thing we got up so early.

Partway up Big Cottonwood Canyon, our Scoutmaster pulled the car off the side of the highway. We opened the trunk, put on our packs, and started down a narrow dirt road. A sign at the trailhead said: "Lake Blanche, 5 Miles." Although we wouldn't admit it, we were a little nervous, because of what the older Scouts had told us. I'm sure you know how loving, kind, and encouraging older Scouts are to younger Scouts in the troop, right? They said things like, "You're wimps, you're gonna hate it, you're gonna get huge blisters and pass out." We thought hard and came up with brilliant seventh-grader responses like, "Uh-uh."

When we saw the sign, we took a deep breath, tightened the straps on our packs, and prepared to begin the five-mile trek. After the first few minutes of hiking, we began to calm down. The first part of the trail was like walking along the sidewalk. It was smooth and straight and easy. After a while we really began to think backpacking wasn't that hard. We were talking, joking, and chucking pine cones at each other like a typical bunch of obnoxious Scouts. But after crossing a bridge over the creek, the trail went up, and I mean *up,* the side of the mountain. We all just stood there and looked at it, like, "Is that the trail?" "Yeah, that's the trail." "Go ahead," "I'm not goin' first, you go ahead," "I'm not goin' first, you go." Finally, after we got the order figured out, we started up the side of the mountain. It was like climbing stairs with a backpack. The fun and games were over, and now, everyone was quiet. I started to ask myself things like, "Do I like Scouts?" "Where's the lake?" "Why did I think this was going to be fun?"

Finally, one Scout had had enough. He sat down on a rock and announced, "I can't go another step." He looked sick and was panting like he'd just run a mile. The Scoutmaster looked at him, looked at us, then looked at him again. Finally, he said, "I'm going to take him back down the trail and drive him home." Then he looked at us and said, "You guys follow the trail up to the top, and I'll join you sometime later tonight."

Another half-hour of hiking had not gone by when another Scout complained in almost the same words: "I can't go another step." I guess it was contagious.

It was time for a troop meeting. The seven of us remaining decided the only way we could beat the mountain was if we took it a little bit at a time. We'd take a hundred steps, then rest for a minute, then take another hundred, then rest for a minute, and so on. What a dumb idea. It takes a long time to go five miles a hundred baby steps at a time. It was like playing "Mother, May I" for three hours.

We trudged on. The sun set, and it began to get dark. I was afraid I'd burn out my batteries, so I used the light from the flashlights around me to help me see the trail . We'd hike, then we'd rest, then we'd hike, then we'd rest. The trail was rocky and steep, and we all began to wonder, "Is this the right trail? Where's the lake? Maybe we're lost."

Another couple of hours went by, and I remember coming across something very strange. I saw stars, but they were on the ground. Not being real intelligent, I just stared at them for a few seconds, trying to figure out what was going on. Finally a ripple rolled through the stars, and my brain kicked in—"John, this could be a reflection." Suddenly, I realized I was standing a foot away from the shallow northern end of Lake Blanche! I had almost led my Scout troop right into the water. Can you imagine the headlines? "Seven Scouts Drown While Trying to Build Underwater Campfire—Investigators Wonder: Were They Brain Dead?"

As we started to unload our packs, we quickly learned why our tired Scout had had such a hard time. He opened his flap, and the first thing he took out was a huge can of Dinty Moore beef chunk stew. Then he took out an industrial-size can of Nalley's chili con carne, and another can of Dinty Moore beef chunk stew. He had enough food in his pack for a ward activity. The rest of us were standing together with our jaws dropped as he unloaded his personal, two-year, food-storage program in the dirt. He had also packed three different flashlights (each with heavy batteries) and three canteens full of water, not to mention the essentials, like a tent and sleeping bag.

He had loaded his pack with things that were too heavy, that he didn't need, and that made the hike a lot harder than it needed to be. I tried to be smarter than that. The night before the hike, I asked my older brother (one of the older Scouts in the troop) what I should take, and after listening to his wise counsel, I packed a half a bag of Cheerios, and a canteen. Fortunately for me, I caught some fish the next morning, and for breakfast, lunch, and dinner, I had fish, Cheerios, and water. It sounds bad, but when you're camping, you'll eat anything. If you drop your fish on the ground, you pick it up and say, "Mmm, mountain flavor Shake and Bake." If you try to boil water, and it gets ashes in it, you say, "Mmm, makes your hot chocolate crunchy."

Here's my point: there are two things that make backpacking

hard. One is how steep the trail is. The other is what we put in our pack. We cannot change the *trail,* but we can make the hike a lot easier if we change what we put in our *pack*!

Life is like backpacking. We begin each morning with an empty backpack, but as soon as we get to the mirror, some of us begin to load up. We say, "No way, I am so ugly" and drop in a rock, *clunk.* We say, "I am so fat" and drop in another, *clunk.* We say, "I'm not popular," and another rock hits the pile. Soon, our pack is so full of rocks we can hardly make it out the front door, then we ask something really brilliant: "Why is life so hard?" Well, life *is* hard, but we make it a lot worse when we load up our packs with stuff that is too heavy, that we don't need, and that makes the hike harder than it needs to be.

The trail of life is rough—it will throw you twists and turns you can't possibly anticipate—we cannot change the trail. But again, we can make the hike easier if we will *change what's in our pack.* What are you carrying in *your* backpack?

Let me suggest three things to help us find the rocks in our packs and throw them out! The first is simply to understand who we are. This is nothing new. We've sung "I Am a Child of God" a hundred times. The Young Women stand up each week and say, "We are daughters of a Heavenly Father who loves us, and we love Him . . ." We sing songs about it, we read scriptures about it, and we talk about it in seminary. But we must, at some time, understand what it really means to be a child of God.

When I was on my mission in the Philippines, my companion and I were given a referral for a seventy-five year old man named Johnny Sajonas. He was frustrated with religion and was bordering on atheism. We approached his home and knocked on the post of his fence just outside the door. A partially bearded old man with a cane in his hand and a frown on his face appeared. He asked what we wanted. We told him that we were missionaries from The Church of Jesus Christ of Latter-day Saints and that we wanted to share a message with him about the Lord and about prophets.

He stood silently, examining us from head to foot for a moment, and then said, "You're very young. I doubt you can teach me anything." I was a bit surprised, but I smiled and responded, "Oh, sir, we have great confidence in our message. Please let us come back and share it with you." He took a minute to think about it and finally mumbled, without changing his tone or his expression in the least, "You come back tomorrow at ten o'clock." Then he turned and walked into the house.

The next day when we arrived at Brother Sajonas's house, he invited us inside, and we sat down on a bamboo bench in front of his Nestle's Quick table (that's what we call a coffee table in the Church). We started out, as was customary at that time, with the discussion on the restoration of the Church. As Elder Warren began to teach, we noticed that our investigator was rather anxious and fidgety. He'd look at the floor, then at the ceiling, then off to the side. You had to be a gymnast to keep eye contact! And he didn't seem to be listening to what we were saying.

After a few moments, he interrupted us in midsentence, looked straight at me, and asked in an angry tone, "Who created evil?" We sat there for a moment in shock. Then I cleared my throat and responded like any good senior companion, "Well . . . uh . . . you see, it's uh . . . uh . . . Elder Warren, you wanna take that one?" Just then I understood his *real* question—did *God* create evil? I picked up my Bible and said, "Sir, it has to do with a place called the premortal existence," and I began to explain. I doubt he'd ever heard anything like it before, since the belief in a pre-earth life is rather unique to our church. I referred to the book of Isaiah and told him about Lucifer, the son of the morning, who, by his own choice, rebelled against God and fell from heaven, becoming the father of lies and the father of evil. Our investigator just sat for a second, then nodded slowly as if to say, "Okay . . . I'll buy that for now." I hoped I had answered him correctly, and I felt relieved that he was satisfied with our response.

We tried to continue where we had left off in the Restoration discussion, but again our investigator was off in another world. He stopped us in midsentence again and loudly demanded, "Why are there so many wars?"

"Uh . . . well, you see, it's uh . . . uh . . . Elder Warren, you wanna . . ." The answer came again, "You see, sir, it has to do with something we received in the premortal existence. It's called agency." I explained how people have a hard time getting along with one another, and that this is true about the leaders of our countries as well. Sometimes we don't do a very good job of running this world, and we get in fights and in wars. But if God came down and solved all our problems, we wouldn't be able to learn and grow, and that's what life is for. This answer seemed to get him thinking, and we continued with our discussion.

He waited a minute and then stopped us a third time and asked, "Why do so many children starve?" What a good question! Elder Warren and I had seen things in the Philippines that we'd never seen before. Malnutrition and poverty were almost everywhere we looked. Little kids, really little, some not even old enough to walk, would crawl and play around ditches that were actually open sewers. Some had parasites in their bodies that would stunt their growth. Others had patchy rashes on their heads that would make their hair fall out. Some had open cuts and wounds that weren't properly cleaned and dressed and never seemed to heal. I had asked myself the same question. I had heard it explained once in Sunday School, and I tried to explain it to Brother Sajonas. "Heavenly Father has a different perspective than we do. When we see a child die, that's how we see it—a child dying. Heavenly Father, on the other hand, sees one of his own spirit children being set free and coming home to him after being away for only a short time."

Finally, it dawned on us that we were teaching the wrong lesson. For every question he asked, the answer came from the plan of salvation. We should have been teaching the Purpose of Life discussion!

The introductory visual aid for that discussion listed three questions. I turned to it and began to explain. A change of expression came over his face, and I watched him in silence as he read and reread each question:

Where did I come from?

Why am I here?

Where will I go when I die?

His eyes moistened, and tears fell from his face. I had never seen this reaction to this picture or any other in my flip chart, and I didn't know what was going on. I looked at Elder Warren and then at Brother Sajonas, and just then the Spirit seemed to whisper, "Elder, testify." I sat forward on the edge of the bench, looked in Brother Sajonas's eyes, and testified to him that we knew where we came from, why we were here, and where we were going. He sat silent for a moment. Then he stood up, motioned for us to wait, and walked slowly into the back of the room. He picked a little red book from the shelf and made his way back to where we were sitting. Then he opened up the book to the back inside cover, held it up in front of my face, and said tearfully, "You are so young!" He had written some things on the back inside cover. In his shaky old handwriting, it said:

My Eternal Questions:

1. Where did I come from?

2. Why am I here?

3. What do I need to accomplish?

4. Where will I go when I die?

After I read the words, I looked up into his tear-filled eyes as he said, "You are so young. And you've come from so far to teach me these things."

The next day we placed the entire plan of salvation on the table for him with cardboard visual aids. I remember watching Brother Sajonas bow his head, cover his face with his hands, and sob, "I have been looking for this for forty years." Brother Sajonas was an engineer, an educated man, but even after all his schooling, he didn't know who he was, where he was from, and what God expected him to do. But one day, a couple of nineteen-year-olds walked in and told him all about it.

Now I'd like to talk to you. You are so young. And yet you know where you come from, why you're here, and where you're going. Why do you know? Why have you been given the privilege when there are billions of people in this world who don't know? Many of them are miserable and frustrated like Brother Sajonas, who are "only kept from the truth because they know not where to find it" (D&C 123:12).

I remember as a teenager sitting in firesides and youth conferences and hearing speaker after speaker say, "You're a child of God," and I would think, *Big deal, isn't everyone? Why should that make me feel so good?* What, then, does it mean to be a child of God? Why is it talked about so much? Being a child of God means that God is intensely interested in us and in our progress. He wants us back. His work is to bring to pass our immortality and eternal life. Someone who truly knows who he or she is would never think of doing things like drinking, doing drugs, or being immoral. I think every time our knees hit the floor, we should ask Heavenly Father to help us understand who we are. Perhaps you have the privilege of knowing who *you* are so that you can tell everyone else in the world who *they* are. Every person on this earth is a child of God, but not every person knows it. We do, but if we are truly a chosen generation, that means we have work to do. Being chosen doesn't mean you sit on a throne to be admired. If we're really chosen, it's because we've been chosen to *work*. Part of that work is helping each other make progress on this backpacking trip called life.

Sometimes we have to help each other a step at a time. A second step in lightening our load as we trudge onward and upward is to decide to be a "builder" instead of a "wrecker." It's a lot easier to tear people down than to build them up.

We can choose whether to be either a builder or a wrecker. We can sit in our Sunday School, Mutual, or school classes and say, "This is boring" Or we can say, "What can I do to make this a better class?" We have our agency. We can criticize, complain, and cut people down, or we can build, bolster, and brighten the lives of those around us.

A few years ago, I taught at a youth conference at San Diego State University. On the afternoon of the first Monday, the participants were coming into the cafeteria for lunch. Three very large young men, each about the size of a major appliance, entered the cafeteria. Once they had loaded their trays with food, they turned and looked around the cafeteria for a place to sit. They could've sat just about anywhere they wanted because no one would have dared complain, but they spotted a table in the back occupied by one young man who was barely old enough to attend the conference. The three of them turned and headed in that direction.

Now what would you think? Here are these three tough guys heading toward the table of a little kid. The counselors at the table thought these three were going to give this kid a bad time, and they were preparing to come to his defense. Imagine our surprise when one of these large young men, seventeen-year-old Jerry, put his hand on the shoulder of the boy at the table and politely asked if they could eat with him. The boy nodded his head that they could join him (as if he would have said no), and these three wonderful young men sat down, ate their lunch, and made friends with him. I believe that angels in the room were doing high fives. (I don't know exactly how angels rejoice. Maybe they just look down and exclaim, "Thou art cool.") I don't believe Jerry himself understood what a "Chosen Generation" thing he had just done. Why was he able to do that? What made him able to be nice to someone when it would have been easier to just ignore him?

I believe it was because Jerry had worked on point number one—

he knew who he was. He knew that he didn't have to talk only to the people who looked like him, or dressed like him, or who played the same sports that he did, or who could bench press a Toyota like he could, but he could talk to anyone, and be their friend. He knew that it was nice to be important, but more important to be nice. Jerry was a builder. President Spencer W. Kimball once said: "The Lord does notice us, and he watches over us, but it is usually through another person that he meets our needs (*New Era,* March 1981, 47).

Jerry became that "other person" Heavenly Father used to help meet the needs of another. Jesus taught, "If ye love them which love you, what reward have ye? do not even the publicans the same? And if ye salute your brethren only, what do ye more than others? do not even the publicans so? Be ye therefore perfect, even as your Father which is in heaven is perfect" (Matthew 5:46–48). In other words, if you're only nice to the people that are nice to you, big deal. If you only say "hi" to those that say "hi" to you, what are you doing more than anyone else?

It's easy to love those who love us. The challenge is to love those who are hard to love. You will be amazed at how much lighter your own load will become when you seek to help others lighten their loads. In other words, forget your backpack for a while and help others lighten theirs. Somehow, your own backpack becomes lighter when you forget about it and focus on lightening the load of someone else. When you lose yourself in the service of others, you find yourself (see Matthew 16:25; Mosiah 2:17).

The third thing we can do to lighten our load is best explained by an experience I had once at a youth camp. Some young women had disappeared during an activity and failed to show up that night at the curfew hour. When they finally did return, we could tell that they had been drinking. One of the rules of the conference was that participants must follow the standards of the Church or they would be sent home.

I sat down with one of these young women at about one o'clock in the morning, and we began to talk. She was embarrassed about what she had done and kept her head down and her eyes on the floor. We talked for quite a while about her interests and background, and when I felt that she knew I wasn't going to give her a big lecture, I began to ask her some questions. (I'll call her Aimee, although that's not her real name.)

"Could I be your big brother for a minute?" (This happened long enough ago that I could have been her big brother)

"Uh-huh."

"Aimee, do you want to be good?" (I think that's a great question because everyone is born with the Light of Christ.)

"Yeah, I guess so."

"Aimee, do you pray?"

"No."

"When was the last time you prayed?"

"Well, I give opening prayers in seminary or I bless the food, but I don't mean anything by it."

"Why not?"

The next thing she said was the classic rock in the backpack that is *most common* among youth I've worked with. She said: "Well, I've made some mistakes, and I don't feel comfortable praying. I don't see why Heavenly Father would listen to me because I've done so many dumb things."

This belief is the most common but the most difficult of problems to overcome. Every time I've shared this story, I've had young people tell me that they've felt just like Aimee. Once Satan convinces us that there's no turning back, we may stop praying or reading the scriptures or doing the things that bring happiness and the Spirit of the Lord into our lives.

Often we don't understand that the times we feel least like praying are when we need to pray the most. Saying that you don't want to pray because you feel unworthy is like saying that you don't want to see a doctor because you don't feel well.

Nephi said, "If ye would hearken unto the Spirit which teacheth a man to pray ye would know that ye must pray; for the evil spirit teacheth not a man to pray, but teacheth him that he must not pray" (2 Nephi 32:8). If you've felt like you shouldn't pray, you've listened to the instructions of the wrong spirit! Heavenly Father always wants you to pray.

Prayer is a powerful tool for solving problems. Elder Thomas S. Monson once said: "Prayer can solve more problems, alleviate more suffering, prevent more transgression, and bring about greater peace and contentment in the human soul than can be obtained in any other way" (See *Ensign,* October 1991, 2).

As uncomfortable as we may sometimes feel, as unworthy as we may feel, even when we know we've done wrong, we can be assured that there is someone who will always be there and who will always be willing to listen.

Bishop H. Burke Peterson has said: "I want you to know that I know that whenever one of Heavenly Father's children kneels and talks to him, he listens. I know this as well as I know anything in this world—that Heavenly Father listens to every prayer from his children. I know our prayers ascend to heaven. No matter what we may have done wrong, he listens to us" ("Prayer—Try Again," *Ensign,* June 1981, 73).

I spent a couple of hours trying to convince Aimee that although she felt uncomfortable, she needed to pray. Aimee did pray that night, a simple prayer, but it was a start. I remember feeling that Aimee had made quite a turnaround.

Later on I started having doubts. How could one prayer on one night change a life around—especially when this had been going on for months? Sure, people can change, but they usually don't. The next morning Aimee went home, and we continued with the youth conference. More than six months passed, and I received a letter from Aimee. She wrote: "Hey, buddy, how are things going? Everything seems to be just fine with me. I have come to realize how important it is to obey the commandments. I have been praying and reading scriptures—my life has totally changed. I don't even hang around the so-called cool people that drink. It's not worth it—they are not true friends. Guess what, I got my patriarchal blessing. That also helps me to be good. It encourages me a lot. I now know that life isn't just one big party. I love ya! Aimee." Aimee learned to pray, and she and her Heavenly Father turned her life around.

We have learned that man is that he might have joy, and yet many of us seem to insist on keeping the rocks in our backpacks by refusing to understand that the Lord really loves us and will help us when we need to repent and change.

If we are to lighten our load, we must understand who we are. We must understand the identity of those around us and build them up. And, as Aimee discovered, we must strive to be worthy. Of all the stuff we carry around, nothing is heavier than unrepented sin

Yes, life is hard, and the trail does not get much easier. But we can make the hike easier by emptying our backpacks, by building and serving one another, and by praying and repenting of our sins and striving to keep our lives clean along the way.

Let the Light of the World help you lighten your load. When things get really heavy, and you're tired and weary, remember the words of the Savior: "Come unto me, all ye that labour and are heavy laden, and I will give you rest. Take my yoke upon you, and learn of me; for I am meek and lowly in heart: and ye shall find rest unto your souls. For my yoke is easy, and my burden is light" (Matthew 11:28–30).

John Bytheway is from Salt Lake City, Utah. He served his mission in the Philippines, and later graduated from Brigham Young University. He is currently finishing up his master's degree in religious education at BYU, and working as an administrator at Deseret Book Company. John and his wife, Kimberly, have three children.

4

THE DATING YEARS: CHARTING A SAFE COURSE

Randal A. Wright

When I was about thirteen years old, our family took a vacation in the West, on which the highlight of the trip was touring Carlsbad Caverns in New Mexico. My cousin and I couldn't wait to enter the cave. Seeing our eagerness to explore *all* the 640 acres open to visitors, my father decided to stay above while we went the 829 feet down to the floor of the caverns.

Our guide gave us interesting details of the interior of the cave. Since he had the only light, we stayed real close to him at first. He pointed out dangers along the trail and the bats inhabiting the cave, repeatedly warning us to stay on the marked paths. As the tour progressed, my cousin and I paid little attention to these warnings and began to lag behind the main group.

At one point of interest, the guide invited the group to gather in close to him. We two were off down the trail and didn't hear him. He said he would turn the lights off to let us see how dark the caverns are. When he flipped the switch, we found ourselves enveloped in a darkness like no other. It frightened me badly, especially knowing we were away from the safety of our guide. I was never more relieved than when he switched the lights back on. We stayed much closer to the guide for the rest of the tour. When our journey through the cavern was over, I was very happy to see my father again as we came to the surface.

One of the most successful tools Satan uses in our day to keep us from accomplishing our earthly missions is immorality. He throws many temptations in our way and would enjoy seeing us stumble and fall. His is a life of darkness and misery (as in the cave), and he desires company.

But our loving Heavenly Father has offered us a special guide who has safety rules for us to follow so we can have successful dating experiences during our teenage years. These guidelines have been repeatedly stated by our latter-day prophets and are available for us to read and follow. They provide the help we need to withstand Satan's temptings. By following the prophet, we are not left in the dark. These inspired rules from our prophets mark a bright path to true happiness and can lead to a temple marriage, with fun in dating and socializing along the way.

Some of you may ask, "What does a ninety-two-year-old man know about the teenage dating scene of today, since he hasn't dated in over seventy years?" Well, that question is a lot like asking a master mechanic with seventy years experience what he knows about changing the spark plugs in a car. During their years in the Lord's service, our prophets have dealt with thousands of cases of immorality. But our prophet has far greater insight than experience only. He receives direct inspiration and revelation from the Lord. The Lord and his prophet want us to be truly happy. With that in mind, let's look at a few guidelines that, if followed, will help you chart a safe course through the dating years.

Keep good company. "Be careful in the selection of your friends. If in the presence of certain persons you are lifted to nobler heights, you are in good company. But if your friends or associates encourage base thoughts, then you had best leave them" (Ezra Taft Benson, *God, Family, Country* [Salt Lake City: Deseret Book Co., 1974], 241).

The word *company* does not mean only your friends or associates. Television, movies, music, and books we read can also be friend or foe. The places we choose to enter can influence us for good or bad. We must stay on the marked path, the one that will make us feel happy forever, not gratified for just a moment.

No dating until age sixteen, and then only double or group dating. For many years the Church has tried diligently to discourage youth from early dating and also from single dating until the proper time. "Group social activities should be provided as alternatives to early dating or to activities that encourage teenagers to pair off. . . . Some youth who do pair off exclusively in their early teens are emotionally and socially immature. That is one reason why the Church counsels youth to date only after age 16, and even then not to pair off exclusively with one partner" (*Young Women Handbook*, 1988, 20). Here again, when we place ourselves in situations that we have been counseled against, we risk disaster.

Many are confused about what a *date* actually is. I have discussed this subject many times with my seminary and institute students. They had different answers and opinions, but finally we came up with a definition that everyone agreed with. A date means a pairing off with one person for the duration of an activity. A date does not necessarily mean the formal process of a boy calling a girl, asking her to go somewhere for a specific time, then driving to her home to pick her up. There are formal dates as well as informal or casual dates. Here are some case studies. You decide (honestly) whether each would be defined as a date or not:

1. A fourteen-year-old young woman invites a fifteen-year-old young man to a stake dance. They are together all evening, not dancing with anyone else. Is this a date?

President Spencer W. Kimball had this to say about dances: "For a youth to dance all evening with one partner, which we might call 'monopolistic' dancing, is not only antisocial but it circumscribes one's legitimate pleasures and opportunities. Also it can encourage improper intimacies by its exclusiveness" (*The Miracle of Forgiveness* [Salt Lake City: Bookcraft, 1969], 222).

2. A thirteen-year-old boy asks a girl of the same age to meet him at a high school homecoming game. Since he cannot drive, his parents take him. He buys the girl a corsage; she buys him a boutonniere. They are together for the duration of the game and are seen holding hands. Both say this is not a date. What do you say?

A young woman in one of my institute classes said, "I think what the prophet is telling us is that we shouldn't be pairing off with anyone before the proper time." Some may still question why the prophet has counseled our teens not to date until age sixteen when all their school friends are allowed to. I have found no better evidence to back this counsel than that provided by two Utah researchers. The findings from their five-year study on teen pregnancy are unmistakable. They polled 2,200 teenagers in New Mexico, Utah, Arizona, and California. Of the girls who had begun dating at age twelve, 91 percent had sexual relations before graduating from high school. Of the girls who started dating at age thirteen, the number was 56 percent. Of those who began dating at age fourteen, the number was 53 percent, and of those who began dating at age fifteen, the number was 40 percent. But of the young women who waited until sixteen to begin dating, only 20 percent were sexually active before high school graduation (see *Church News,* September 10, 1988, 16).

Pairing off at such a young age presents a very real moral danger for the future. "The recreational and social activities of the crowd can be wholesome and entertaining. Physical and moral safety is increased in the multiplicity of friends" (*The Miracle of Forgiveness,* 221).

Don't place yourself in the position where the chance of being immoral is greatly increased. Double or group dating after age sixteen, with a variety of different people, increases one's safety and is also much more fun!

Date only worthy members of the Church. Remember the importance of proper dating. President Kimball gave some wise counsel on this subject: "Clearly, right marriage begins with right dating. . . . Therefore, this warning comes with great emphasis. Do not take the chance of dating nonmembers, or members who are untrained and faithless. [You] may say, 'Oh, I do not intend to marry this person. It is just a "fun" date.' But one cannot afford to take a chance on falling in love with someone who may never accept the gospel" (*The Miracle of Forgiveness,* 241–42).

"Our Heavenly Father wants you to date young women who are faithful members of the Church, who encourage you to serve a full-time mission and to magnify your priesthood" (Ezra Taft Benson, *Ensign,* May 1966, 45).

I have heard several questions and comments about this counsel. Why would the prophet come out so strongly about this subject in general conference? First of all, let's remember that this is not just the prophet's counsel. He appears to be relaying a message to us. His statement reads, "Our Heavenly Father wants you to date young women who are faithful members of the Church." So, actually, the question should be, Why does Heavenly Father feel this to be so important?

What is wrong with dating nonmembers as long as it's just for fun? Very few marriages occur without the couple first having a fun date. The old saying "You marry who you date" is literally true in our society.

What if you live in an area where there are few worthy members to date? This can be a real challenge. Make sure you attend all your Young Men and Young Women activities, youth conferences, and other stake events. They will provide opportunities to meet LDS youth from other areas.

What about missionary work? Presidents Benson and Kimball are two of the greatest missionaries of our time. They definitely would not discourage missionary work but would instead endorse the right way to do it. We can still have group activities that non-members are invited to, without pairing off. It is possible to have fun with our nonmember friends and do missionary work while following the prophet's counsel.

No going steady during the teen years. "A vicious, destructive, social pattern of early steady dating must be changed," wrote Elder Spencer W. Kimball. "It is my considered feeling, having had some experience in interviewing youth, that the change of this one pattern of social activities of our youth would immediately eliminate a majority of the sins of our young folks" ("Save the Youth of Zion," *Improvement Era,* September 1965, 806).

Why would not going steady help keep a youth on a safe course through the dating years? Going steady seems to promise a secure relationship, a date every weekend, someone to care about. At least that's the way it sometimes seems to young people. But here are some reasons for *not* going steady:

1. Going steady prior to a mission can interfere with a young man's decision to serve and with a missionary's effectiveness once he is serving. President Ezra Taft Benson advised: "Avoid steady dating with a young man prior to the time of his mission call. If your relationship with him is more casual, then he can make that decision to serve more easily and also can concentrate his full energies on his missionary work instead of the girlfriend back home." ("To the Young Women of the Church," *Ensign,* November 1986, 82–83).

2. Their circle of friendships is limited when young people go steady. They usually limit the opportunity of meeting new people and developing new friendships. To develop our personalities, we all need interaction with many people in social settings. Going steady limits this interaction, without which a person lacks the social exposure to make a wise decision on a marriage partner when the time comes.

3. Jealousy and insecurity increase. Young couples become tied

down and restricted. One girl commented, "Instead of going steady, I wound up staying home steady because of his jealousy." Oftentimes teens are too young to handle the strong emotions they feel with a steady partner. Many constantly worry about who that partner is talking to or where he or she is going.

Most become extremely possessive of the partner. Courting during the teen years is filled with doubts and apprehensions. Why is she looking at him? Is she prettier than I am? Will we marry? With the maturity arrived at when the proper time for courting comes (after missions for young men), doubts leave and certainty replaces jealousy. Most steadies become very preoccupied. They think of their steady almost constantly during their waking hours. Schoolwork, seminary, scripture study, and even household chores often suffer. It often becomes difficult for some teens to even carry on a conversation without the boyfriend's or girlfriend's name coming up. At a time when youth should be thinking about schoolwork, developing talents, homemaking skills, and mission preparation, many are spending almost every waking hour thinking about love and marriage. It is not courtship but friendship that should be the relationship between teenagers.

4. Immorality and early marriages increase. One family researcher has defined going steady as "acting like you are already married while still living at your parents' home." Going steady tends to give the young man a sense of familiarity or ownership, and to the young woman a feeling of belonging to someone—just as in marriage! This greatly increases the chances of their becoming immoral.

The rising incidence of teen pregnancy is frightening. How many of these young girls were going steady at the time they became pregnant? The number one reason for early marriage, according to research, is pregnancy. The number two reason is early dating.

5. Family life becomes disrupted when a teen goes steady. Too

often the boy is either over at the girl's house or on the phone with her—or they are out together. A teenager who is going steady often does not want to do much with his or her own family.

Oftentimes youth, and even their parents, deny they are going steady when it is obvious that they are. If a ring or other token of promise is not involved, then they are just "good friends," even if they date only each other and talk about getting married. If a boy and girl are exclusively paired off, a ring does not need to be involved— they are going steady.

President Spencer W. Kimball has said, "Young men and women, not yet ready for marriage, should be friends with many others, but they should not engage in courting" (Edward L. Kimball, ed., *The Teachings of Spencer W. Kimball* [Salt Lake City: Bookcraft, 1982], 288). The benefits of not going steady during the teen years are great.

Do not kiss improperly. "Kissing has been prostituted and has degenerated to develop and express lust instead of affection, honor, and admiration. To kiss in casual dating is asking for trouble. What do kisses mean when given out like pretzels and robbed of sacredness? What is miscalled the 'soul kiss' is an abomination and stirs passions to the eventual loss of virtue. Even if timely courtship justifies the kiss, it should be a clean, decent, sexless one like the kiss between mother and son, or father and daughter" (*The Teachings of Spencer W. Kimball,* 281).

Kissing should mean something special. Usually when a young man kisses a girl, he gives the message that he likes her a lot. Unfortunately, some boys are only playing games with the girl, and feelings can be hurt as a result.

Several years ago I heard about a young man who claimed to hold the record in his stake for kissing the most girls in one day. According to reports, he had kissed six different girls that day and was very proud of this feat. This seemed unusual to me, so I looked forward to a casual conversation with him to discuss his dating practices.

One day the opportunity came. After we had visited for a while, the subjects of dating and, finally, kissing came up. I asked about his ideas on kissing. He let me know that he thought he should kiss as many girls as possible before his mission, to see if he was compatible with any. I asked him how many girls he had kissed. His response: "So many that I can't keep count! In fact, I really don't believe if they all walked through the door right now I would even recognize them all." I was surprised but smiled so he'd keep talking. I finally asked, "How many in one day?" "Six," came the quick reply, "and that was all before 2:00 P.M. I stayed with the same girl after that for the rest of the day." He told me that he was at a high school event when this took place. I asked if the girls were LDS. He slowly shook his head but quickly added that it wasn't a date.

I asked him if he had ever heard what President Kimball had taught on the subject of kissing. He sheepishly said no.

"Do you want to hear it?" I asked.

"Not really, but go ahead."

I then read him the statement above. His comment was, "Well, I have given out so many pretzels, there is no need to stop now!" We continued to talk, and I asked him if he had anyone in mind to date when he got home from his mission. His answer surprised me. One of the top young women on his list was one that we both knew had set a goal to kiss no one until she was sure they would marry.

The next day when I saw the young man again, I said: "Guess what! Your kissing record has been beaten!"

"No way! I know no one around here has beaten it," came his startled reply.

"Yes, it happened!"

"Who?"

"Your future wife!" I calmly replied. "She had the same goal as you, and kissed seven different nonmember guys in one day."

He looked shocked and said, "But you don't know who my future wife is."

"You're right," I said, "but I'm telling you who you deserve!"

"I guess I do have a double standard, don't I?" he said. "I have never thought of it in that way before."

Immorality does not usually begin with necking or petting. I begins with kissing. Then come sexual thoughts. These grow whenever entertained, until the strong become weak and yield to temptation. To help you prepare for a temple marriage, imagine your future wife or husband doing the identical things you do. This will help you avoid temptations, and then you'll be prepared when the time is right for finding an eternal companion.

Be courteous to your parents. President David O. McKay said: "Parents who do not know where their children are at night are recreant [disloyal] to the sacred obligation of parenthood and untrue to the high ideals of the Church regarding home life" (Conference Report, October 1951, 10).

As a safeguard and also a courtesy, let your parents know where you are going, who you'll be with, and when they can expect you home. Upon your arrival home, sit down with your parents to discuss the evening's activities. This provides great safety. You surely would not feel comfortable discussing your evening if you had done something wrong. I have a friend who told me that his after-date discussions with his mom kept him on the marked path. He had been tempted many times to be immoral, but knowing that he would be talking to his mom about the evening's activities and giving her a good-night kiss kept him clean.

Obedience to our prophet's counsel brings safety and happiness. Our path *is* brightly marked; now we must chart the course we will follow. What will yours be?

THE DATING YEARS: CHARTING A SAFE COURSE

Randal A. Wright is a fifth-generation Texan and serves in the Texas San Antonio Mission presidency. He earned his Ph.D. in family studies at Brigham Young University. He has worked with Especially for Youth for sixteen years and taught at BYU for four years. Currently, Brother Wright is the institute director at the University of Texas at Austin. He is married and has five children. In addition to his family, he loves basketball, Israel, and computers.

5

UNDERSTANDING THE ATONEMENT

Stace Hucks Christianson

It has been some years now since I sat in my living room with the parents of some teenagers and had a discussion about chastity. We talked about the challenges that the royal generation faces and the growing strength of the opposition. Since I hadn't had the experience of raising my own teenagers yet, I sat quietly and mostly listened to the experiences of those loving parents as they voiced their concerns and searched for solutions. They talked about the need for education and clearer boundaries, more firesides, lessons, and youth conferences focused on teaching the law of chastity to the youth of the Church. As I sat there listening, I reflected on the comments that my seminary students often made. "We get so sick of everything being focused on the law of chastity. We've gotten the message; we know when we are living it and we know when we're not." It was then that I asked myself: Why do the adults feel as though the youth aren't getting enough direction and guidelines, while the youth are complaining that they are getting too much?

I went home that night seeking answers to that question. Answers rarely come to me suddenly. I have found that I must be very patient and persistent in my search for truth. So I was not surprised that it took several months to make an important discovery: I was reading in Alma 39, the part where Alma confronts his son

Corianton about the son's immoral behavior. It is interesting that Corianton received more counsel from his father than any of the prophet's other sons. What struck me, though, was that in the four chapters of counsel only a few beginning verses addressed the broken law itself. Most of what Alma had to say was about the Savior and the effect of His atoning sacrifice. As I reflected upon what I had read, I thought about my experiences with my students in seminary, and I realized that what enables us to live righteously is not our devotion to the commandments, but our devotion to Christ. If we love and desire to serve him, keeping his commandments is a joy and not a task.

This reminded me of what Nephi taught: "We know that it is by grace that we are saved, after all we can do. And, notwithstanding we believe in Christ, we keep the law of Moses, and look forward with steadfastness unto Christ, until the law shall be fulfilled. For, for this end was the law given; . . . And we talk of Christ, we rejoice in Christ, we preach of Christ, we prophesy of Christ, and we write according to our prophecies, that our children may know to what source they may look for a remission of their sins. Wherefore, we speak concerning the law that our children may know the deadness of the law; and they, by knowing the deadness of the law, may look forward unto that life which is in Christ, and know for what end the law was given. And after the law is fulfilled in Christ, that they need not harden their hearts against him when the law ought to be done away" (2 Nephi 25:23–27).

This is the kind of devotion that is anchored in an intimate relationship with the Savior, and that kind of devotion makes it easy to put his will and desires first. Those of my students who were succeeding in living righteously were able to do so because at some point they had drawn close to him and experienced a personal outpouring of his love. It followed that they, like Nephi, wanted to return a portion of that love to him. A desire to surrender our rebellious wills to Christ is a characteristic of his disciples. And one of the consequences of such a surrender is a change of heart, something King Benjamin's people experienced after their conversions: "The Spirit of the Lord Omnipotent, which has wrought a mighty change in us, or in our hearts, that we have no more disposition to do evil, but to do good continually" (Mosiah 5:2). (Notice that the change of heart is brought about by "the Spirit of the Lord.")

Again, it was months later that I was reading in the Pearl of Great Price, in the book of Moses, when I noticed that Moses asks the Lord God a very significant question. He says, "Tell me concerning this earth, and the inhabitants thereof, and also the heavens" (Moses 1:36). In other words, what is the Lord's purpose for the inhabitants of the earth? And God answers, "This is my work and my glory—to bring to pass the immortality [to live forever] and eternal life [to live like God and live with him forever] of man" (Moses 1:39). To bring eternal life to us required that several things be accomplished. First, that God create a place where he could send us to experience mortality. Second, the creation of a plan that would provide a way for us to be redeemed from death and sin and become like him. Such a plan would need to provide or preserve knowledge, free agency, opposition (in order to have one of those three we must have the other two; they are inseparable), joy, the ability to procreate, a body, and, eventually, a perfect and resurrected body capable of withstanding God's presence. This plan is called the plan of salvation or the plan of redemption (see Alma 12:33).

One of the reasons I feel such passion toward the things that follow in this chapter is because I love discovering the unchanging truths of the gospel. In our church we have very strong traditions and a rich culture. There are Church policies that can help us and give us guidelines, but they are all subject to change. The doctrines and principles discussed in this chapter are eternal truths, which means they are not subject to change. They must be understood if we are to be saved. You will find them consistent in the eternities. They are the most fundamental aspects of our belief system in the gospel of Christ, and, when studied, the most fascinating and profound.

The Old Testament introduces the three pillars of salvation. The first pillar is the Creation, the second pillar is the Fall, and the third pillar is the Atonement. Consider this series of questions, which I will later answer.

1. What is the purpose of the Creation?
2. What does the Creation have to do with the plan of salvation?
3. How does the Creation affect me daily?
4. What does the Fall have to do with the plan of salvation?
5. How does the Fall affect me daily?
6. What does the Atonement have to do with the plan of salvation?
7. How does the Atonement affect me daily?

If you want, you can search for the answers yourself. Look in the following scriptural chapters: 2 Nephi 2; 9 and Alma 12; 40–42.

What is the purpose of the Creation? Heavenly Father created the earth so that we might have a place to live and to work out our salvation by learning to choose good instead of evil. But what about the purpose of *our* creation? When Christ appeared to the Nephites he asked them, "What manner of men ought ye to be? Verily I say unto you, even as I am" (3 Nephi 27:27). The purpose of our creation is to eventually become like Heavenly Father and his Son Jesus Christ, in other words, perfect (see Matthew 5:48; 3 Nephi 12:48). As mentioned earlier, knowledge, free agency, and opposition are all vital components in the process of eternal progression.

What does the Creation have to do with the plan of salvation? When Satan tempted Eve in the Garden of Eden, he told her that if she would partake of the tree of knowledge of good and evil, she would be as the Gods, knowing good and evil, and that she would not die as a consequence. Like many of Satan's lies, it was only half a lie. It was true that if Eve partook of the fruit she would gain knowledge, but it was a lie that she would not die. As a consequence of their disobedience, she and Adam became partakers of two kinds of death. The first is a physical death. Both Eve and Adam had possessed immortal bodies in the Garden of Eden. When they transgressed and were cast out, their bodies became mortal or subject to physical death. The second death was a spiritual death. Spiritual death occurs when we are separated from God, and it happened for Adam and Eve when they were cast out of God's presence. Believing it was the only way to acquire wisdom and knowledge, Eve had partaken (see Moses 4:9–12), and Adam, having committed himself to stay with Eve, also partook of the forbidden fruit. Adam and Eve and their posterity consequently became subject to physical death and were introduced into an environment of increased opposition where they could exercise their agency and acquire knowledge.

How does the Creation affect me daily? People can't exercise agency unless they are capable of making choices. A person can't make choices without encountering opposition. To have knowledge is to understand the full range of choices, and to exercise wisdom is to make a good choice.

Because of their limited experience (thus limited knowledge, limited opposition, and limited ability to exercise their agency), Adam and Eve could never be like God. They were too limited or ignorant. The Lord told Joseph Smith, "It is impossible for a man to be saved in ignorance" (D&C 131:6). So we know that those three principles are key to our salvation. Every day I am on this earth I experience opposition, which gives me the opportunity to exercise my knowledge in making choices. Every day I hope my choices help me progress toward becoming like God (see 2 Nephi 2:11–19).

What does the Fall have to do with the plan of salvation? Eve gives us the answer in Moses 5:11: "Were it not for our transgression we never should have had seed, and never should have known good and evil, and the joy of our redemption, and the eternal life which God giveth unto all the obedient." Was this all a part of God's plan? Yes. Moses 4:6 says, "And [Satan] sought also to beguile Eve, for he knew not the mind of God, wherefore he sought to destroy the world." This scripture teaches us that God's purposes will never be frustrated (see also D&C 3:1–3). Eve explains that the Fall was necessary so that she and Adam could exercise agency and choose to have joy and children. In their state of innocence, Adam and Eve had neither joy nor sorrow (see 2 Nephi 2:11) because they did not have opposition. They also would have had no children until after the Fall (see 2 Nephi 2:23).

How does the Fall affect me daily? The scriptures tell us that while here on earth we are in a state of probation (see 2 Nephi 2:21). We are exposed to wickedness and righteousness, misery and happiness, and other opposites. After experiencing happiness we can continue to make decisions to maintain that happiness and peace of mind or not. One of the benefits of being separated from God is that no one is standing over our shoulder, pressuring us to choose God. We are free to make decisions, and in this we can feel our agency in practice.

What does the Atonement have to do with the plan of salvation? Everything. The Atonement makes all of the aforementioned things possible. Without it we couldn't have opposition, agency, or knowledge. We would have only darkness and despair. Satan's plan did not include agency: "Behold, here am I, send me, I will be thy son, and I will redeem all mankind, that one soul shall not be lost, and surely I will do it; wherefore give me thine honor. . . . Satan rebelled against me [the Father], and sought to destroy the agency of man" (Moses 4:1–3). Satan wanted to control, dominate, and oppress us all.

How does the Atonement affect me daily? The answer to this is one of the most profound truths of the gospel. The Book of Mormon teaches that if there had been no infinite sacrifice made, Satan would be our ruler.

We can only imagine the misery that would be involved were we to be in Satan's power: "For behold, if the flesh should rise no more our spirits must become subject to that angel who fell from before the presence of the Eternal God, and became the devil, to rise no more. And our spirits must have become like unto him, and we become devils, angels to a devil, to be shut out from the presence of our God, and to remain with the father of lies, in misery, like unto himself; yea, to that being who beguiled our first parents, who transformeth himself nigh unto an angel of light, and stirreth up the children of men unto secret combinations of murder and all manner of secret works of darkness" (2 Nephi 9:8–9).

The joy of it all is that because of what Christ endured, we needn't succumb to fear and darkness. Rather, we can have happiness, joy, pleasure, and best of all, peace, because we are the beneficiaries of the Atonement Christ so lovingly provided. More amazing still is the fact that everyone has access to these gifts. Everyone who ever lived on this earth will ultimately be resurrected. Thus, death will be eliminated. People who love the Savior and appreciate what he has done for them, people who know of Christ but don't care that he suffered, people who aren't sure he really even existed, and those who have never heard of him will all receive the gift of immortality. All God's children benefit, because he loves us all. Additionally, those who love the Savior and strive to keep his commandments can be redeemed from sin, cleansed, and made candidates for eternal life. All of this because of the Atonement. Does that affect me daily? Yes. And it will affect me throughout eternity as well. Because of that understanding, I may not always have happiness and joy, but I will always have peace—a gift from the Savior and Redeemer of the world.

The Son of God has perfect integrity. So much was his promise worth before the foundation of this world that the salvation of all the earth's inhabitants rested upon his word. I find it impossible to place my faith anywhere else. I also find it impossible to not place my loyalty, my devotion, my trust, my love, and, ultimately, myself in his care. Experience has taught me that he does a far superior job with my life than I do. C. S. Lewis stated: "The Christian way is different: harder, and easier. Christ says, 'Give me all. I don't want so much of your time and so much of your money and so much of your work: I want You. I have not come to torment your natural self, but to kill it. No half-measures are any good. I don't want to cut off a branch here and a branch there [see Alma 22:15–18], I want the whole tree down. I don't want to drill the tooth, or crown it or stop it, but to have it out. Hand over the whole natural self, all the desires which you think innocent as well as the ones you think wicked— the whole outfit. I will give you a new self instead. In fact, I will give you Myself: my own will shall become yours' [see Alma 5:7, 14]" (*Mere Christianity* [New York: Macmillan, 1978], 167).

My Savior hasn't asked me to die for him. He has asked me to live for him, to live up to what he expects of me. I know his goal is that of the Father's: for me to return to him unashamed and with gratitude for the choice. That is my goal as well.

Stace Hucks Christianson served a mission to Holbrook, Arizona, and later taught seminary and institute for six years. She currently teaches at Brigham Young University and is working toward a master's degree in gender issues. She and her husband, Frank, have one child.

6

YOUR DIVINE DESIGN

Scott Anderson

It was Eddie's third birthday. He had been sick for some time, but his young parents had just transported him to a hospital in Los Angeles, a journey of over two days and nights from their home. They thought that the expert medical staff there might be able to help. Dr. Lowman took one look at the medical history, however, and recognized that Eddie had polio. This dreaded disease had already taken many lives and was considered to be extremely contagious. Dr. Lowman shouted at the parents for bringing the child where he could infect others, and in a fit of rage took little Eddie and placed him in isolation.

For the next three days, young Spencer and Camilla were separated from their beautiful little boy. They frequently heard him scream until they believed that his voice would not recover. The only way they could talk to him was through a little crack in the door, and each time they would leave, he would cry out pitifully again (Edward L. Kimball and Andrew E Kimball, Jr., *Spencer W. Kimball* [Salt Lake City: Bookcraft, 1977], 137–38).

While I was serving on a writing committee for the Church, one of my coworkers shared the experience of hearing President Kimball talk about the personal pain he and his wife had experienced in the hospital with Eddie. He described standing at the door, with his hands pressed against the barriers that were holding him away from his son. President Kimball had then commented that he believed Heavenly Father felt just like that sometimes. As we say our prayers and cry, "Father are you there? Do you care? Why do I feel so alone?" How hard it must be for our loving Heavenly Father not to just "step through the veil," embrace us and say, "I am your Father; I will help you. I want to have you home with me again."

In Moses 7:29–33, Enoch is given a vision of what it would be like to go home to our Heavenly Father. As Enoch enters into His presence, he sees Him crying. He asks how it can be that the God of heaven is weeping. The Lord answers Enoch by explaining that He gave men their knowledge and their agency in the Garden of Eden that they might love one another and choose Him, their Father. He then explains that the vast majority of his children are without affection and even hate their own blood. As Enoch witnessed this scene, he wept as well (see Moses 7:41). These scriptural passages testify to us how our Father in Heaven experiences the feelings described by President Kimball, and so much more.

If we will take time not just to read these thoughts but to think deeply about them, I know that the Spirit can help us begin to *feel* their truth. Our Father in Heaven loves us so much more than we can begin to comprehend. We loved him so much more than we can begin to remember. If we could remember, we would know that we came to this earth with the greatest desire to do everything to show him our love and appreciation for all that he is and does. Just stop and try to prayerfully remember. Could we feel what Enoch felt? Could we feel the compelling love of President and Sister Kimball for their little one and then increase it infinitely to try to sense just a tiny part of his love for us? What would we do if we knew?

In Jacob chapter 5, Nephi's brother quotes a profound prophetic allegory from the brass plates. The allegory symbolically describes all those who have promised to follow the Savior, and yet their commitment to their covenants has not been fruitful enough to lead them back to their God. Thus they cannot fill the earth again with good fruit. In the middle of the story, Jacob records an insight that for those who love the Savior is quite touching and even overwhelming. In verse 41 the Lord of the vineyard (the Savior) is weeping as he witnesses the falling away of his people. He then cries in verse 47, "What could I have done more?" This description happens in the allegory after our Savior suffered intimately and infinitely for all of our pain, sickness, suffering, and sin in Gethsemane. This particular scene follows the greatest love ever manifested, being expressed perfectly and eternally for us. This is subsequent to the beatings, the mocking, and the Crucifixion. At this point in the allegory, we are allowed to see him weeping, wanting to know what more he could have done. The narrative shows us the need to recognize that it is we who need to do more. The Lord of the vineyard then sends his servant who has done as the Lord had commanded, and he brought other servants, noting they were few (v. 70). And the Lord said, "Go to, and labor in the vineyard, with your might. For behold, this is the last time that I will nourish my vineyard; for the end is nigh at hand, and the season speedily cometh; and if ye labor with your might with me ye shall have joy in the fruit which I shall lay up unto myself against the time which will soon come" (v. 71).

When is this last time the Lord's servants will nourish and prune his vineyard? Who is that great generation to bring to pass this marvelous work? The Doctrine and Covenants gives us the key. Speaking to those of this dispensation, the Lord states, "Thou art called to prune my vineyard with a mighty pruning, yea, even for the last time" (D&C 24:19; see 39:17; 75:2; 95:4). Are we not the generation to respond to the call to bring his children back?

To understand our sacred stewardship, President James E. Faust shared the following story: "In 1989 there was a terrible earthquake in Armenia that killed over 30,000 people in four minutes. A distraught father went in frantic search of his son. He reached his son's school only to find that it had been reduced to a pile of rubble. But he was driven by his promise to his son, 'No matter what, I'll always be there for you!' He visualized the corner where his son's class-room would be, rushed there, and started to dig through the debris, brick by brick.

"Others came on the scene—the fire chief, then the police—warning him of fires and explosions, and urging him to leave the search to the emergency crews. But he tenaciously carried on digging. Night came and went, and then, in the 38th hour of digging, he thought he heard his son's voice. 'Armand!' he called out. Then he heard, 'Dad!?! It's me, Dad! I told the other kids not to worry. I told 'em that if you were alive, you'd save me and when you saved me, they'd be saved. . . .

"'There are fourteen of us left out of thirty-three. . . . When the building collapsed, it made a wedge, like a triangle, and it saved us.'

"'Come on out, boy!'

"'No, Dad! Let the other kids out first, 'cause I know you'll get me! No matter what, I know you'll be there for me!'

"There are not words that would adequately explore the feelings in this father's heart as he found his son alive—the incredible joy, the long awaited anticipation after so much life-threatening effort to find him. However, how much greater would be the joy inside this father's heart as he heard those selfless words from a frightened child trapped in a concrete tomb for over 38 hours, 'No Dad, let the other kids out first, 'cause I know you'll get me!'" (*Ensign,* April 2001, 46).

How deeply these words reflect the faithful spirit of the youth of this dispensation. You have a destiny so great that the prophets from all ages have written about you. This is a sacred time when a covenant people will rise up and valiantly keep their covenant to bring his children home. We know that he will be there for us, and because we know this, we can be there for others—confidently reaching out to bring them out of the darkness and into the light of truth and life.

We have eternally known that he would always be there for us. It is not a new thing for us to feel his love and have his example be the very power that gives us sufficient strength to be valiant. Elder Jeffrey R. Holland has explained that if we remembered clearly the premortal existence "we could remember that even in the Grand Council of Heaven He loved us and was wonderfully strong, that *we triumphed even there by the power of Christ and our faith in the Blood of the Lamb*" (*Ensign,* October 1995, 90). Now that we are here, victory in the cause of truth will be by the very same power.

Two missionaries in Munich, Germany, knocked on an old wooden door. The lady of the house said something to them that they had not heard for a long time; she said, "Come in!" One of the elders was so startled at her enthusiasm that he quipped, "Do you know who we are?"

She said, "You want to talk about religion, don't you?"

He said, "Yes, we do!"

She said, "Oh, come in! I've been watching you walk around the neighborhood. I'm so excited to have you here! Please, come in to my study."

In the study she sat down behind a large desk and considered the missionaries with a faint smile. Then she pointed to the three doctoral degrees hanging over her head: one in theology, the study of religion; one in philosophy, the study of ideas; and one in European history, specializing in Christianity.

"You see the row of books right here?" The missionaries viewed a well-displayed set of books. "I wrote them all. I am the theology professor at the University of Munich and have been doing this for forty-one years. I would love to talk about religion." Then, almost rubbing her hands together, she asked, "What would you like to discuss?"

The young missionary, seeking inspiration, replied, "We would like to talk about the Book of Mormon."

"I don't know anything about the Book of Mormon."

"Good!"

Twenty minutes later the elders walked out of the room, having presented her a Book of Mormon. Some weeks later the same lady was in a small room filled with people dressed in white.

The well-known theology professor stood up in front of the small congregation of people and said, "Before I am baptized today, I would like to tell you my feelings. In Amos 8:11 it says there will be famine in the last days. Not a famine of food or drink, but a famine of the word of God. I have been in that famine for over seventy years. Why do you think I have three Ph.D.'s? I have been hungering for truth and striving to find it, but I have not been satisfied." She went on to say, "But then a few weeks ago two young men walked into my home. I want you to know that these elders are very nice and wonderful young men, but they didn't convert me. They couldn't. They didn't know enough." Then she smiled and said, "But since that day they came to my door, I have read the Book of Mormon, the Doctrine and Covenants, the Pearl of Great Price, all of James E. Talmage's writings, *Evidences and Reconciliations* by John A. Widtsoe, and twenty-one other volumes of Church doctrine."

She then stated, "I don't think you members of the Church realize what you have." Then in her quiet, powerful way, she said, "After three years of studying philosophy, I have picked up the Doctrine and Covenants and read a few little verses that answered some of the greatest questions that Aristotle and Socrates proposed years ago. When I read those verses, I wept for the years I studied without the foundation of truth. I don't know why I had to wait so long, but I know I will never take these magnificent teachings lightly."

Again she said, "I don't think you members know what you have. Do you understand that the world is in famine? Do you know that the world is starving for what we have? I have been like a starving person being led to a feast. Over the past weeks, I have been able to feast in a way I've never known possible before."

After delivering her powerful message and challenging questions, she ended her testimony with her favorite scripture: "For don't you see? 'The truth shall make you free' (John 8:32). These missionaries do not simply represent membership in the Church; they carry within their hands the power to make the atonement of Jesus Christ a full force in my life. Today I am going in the water and I am going to make covenants with Christ for the first time with proper authority. I have wanted to do this all my life."

We each have a part in an incredible divine design, forseen by the prophets of old, and we are a part of a plan that has greater significance than we have the power to understand. The Savior is relying on us to do his work, to bring his children to him. So many are in darkness and need help to find the fulness of light and truth. This is the last time that he will nourish and prune his vineyard. President Hinckley has said, "Never forget that you were chosen and brought to earth as a child of God for something of importance in his grand design. He expects marvelous things of you!" ("A Chosen Generation," *Ensign,* May 1992, 70). I testify to the truth of this statement. You are part of a great work, and your Father in Heaven will always be there to guide you, help you, and bless you. I know that he loves you and is eternally grateful for all you do to share the gospel of his Son, our Savior and Redeemer, Jesus Christ.

Scott Anderson served a mission to South Germany, and then married Angelle Clark in the Salt Lake Temple. They are the parents of seven children and grandparents of eleven—nine of them boys. Brother Anderson has a Ph.D. in Marriage and Family Therapy from BYU. He has taught for thirty years in the Church Education System, and is a faculty member at the Orem Institute of Religion adjacent to Utah Valley State College. Brother Anderson enjoys home construction projects, writing, running, and making memories with his family. He loves to teach and share his love of the Savior and His gospel. He has been involved in the "Especially for Youth" Program since it began. He and his wife have enjoyed serving as missionary companions in their ward in Bluffdale, Utah.

7

CONTROLLING UNWORTHY THOUGHTS

Brad Wilcox

Could I . . . uh . . ." The dark-haired young man in front of me shifted awkwardly. "I mean, I was wondering . . . if we could talk." I had just finished speaking at a fireside for young people.

"No problem," I assured him. We walked down the meeting-house hall, away from the groups of people still lingering and enjoying refreshments. I had noticed this particular young man during the fireside. He was tall, handsome, and so clean-cut that he looked as if he could be on the cover of the *New Era*.

"It's about what you said in there," he began quietly. "You know, about being worthy. Well . . ." He hesitated. "Well . . . I . . ." He paused again. His averted eyes did little to disguise the tears that were welling. "It's my thoughts." He forced the words out. "Sometimes I just have the worst thoughts. It's my biggest problem." He shrugged his shoulders and sighed. "I don't know. Sometimes, I just feel so . . . so . . ."

"Dirty?" I filled in his blank. He nodded. The tears glistening on his lashes brimmed over.

In the minutes that followed, we talked privately, and my new friend asked several questions. The first was, "Am I normal?"

Inappropriate thoughts are a natural part of being human and a very normal part of growing up. At one time or another, we have all felt a little hypocritical because we know that the thoughts found in our heads are not found in the Family Home Evening manual. At times, many of us have felt that we should "be glad if we could command the rocks and the mountains to fall upon us to hide us" (Alma 12:14) because of our thoughts. We might not even be seeing the movies that are for "mature" audiences, yet at times we're sure that there is an international film festival going on in our heads! We feel embarrassed. We feel weak, small, unworthy, and, like my new friend who came to me after the fireside, we feel a little dirty.

In the *New Era* we read, "You are not morally sick just because bad thoughts sometimes come into your mind. Thoughts are power-ful, and all of us at times have trouble dealing with them" ("Q&A," May 1989, 17).

My friend's next question went something like this: "If I really don't want them, where do evil thoughts come from?" He's right: we don't want evil thoughts. Not many people I know wake up in the morning saying, "My, I wonder what dirty thoughts I'll have today." The thoughts just come without being invited—that's part of the problem.

We see an attractive person of the opposite sex and bells ring inside our heads. We see shorts that are too short and—as sure as Pavlov's dogs—we hear those bells. We hear people tell off-color jokes or twist an innocent phrase to mean something totally unin-tended, and the bells ring. Then the same jokes replay themselves over and over in our minds and it's as if someone has a finger on the doorbell button and is not letting up. I have even read a few choice words here and there on the walls of public rest rooms and have walked away thinking, *Well, I've never really seen it put quite like that before!*

Unbidden thoughts and ideas seem to demand room in our heads even when we have placed the No Vacancy sign in clear view. Like red traffic lights when we're late to church, those thoughts are simply a part of everyday living in this telestial world. President Ezra Taft Benson assures us, "Our accountability begins with how we handle the evil thought immediately *after* it is presented" (*Ensign,* March 1989, 4; emphasis added).

"Then"—my friend asked his next question—"are my evil thoughts sins?" It is an important question. The Savior warned, "Whosoever looketh on a woman to lust after her hath committed adultery with her already *in his heart"* (Matthew 5:28; emphasis added). In Proverbs we read, "As [a man] thinketh *in his heart,* so is he" (23:7; emphasis added). Truman G. Madsen writes: "Reread the oft-quoted passages about the thoughts. You will note that it is not the occurrence of ideas in the head but their lodgment in the heart that degrades. . . . The issue is not so much what thoughts occur in our minds, but how we nurture them in our desires" (*Christ and the Inner Life* [Salt Lake City: Bookcraft, 1978], 35).

Our minds are like rivers, and unworthy thoughts are like birds that swoop down out of nowhere to snatch an unsuspecting fish. If we do all we can to get rid of the pesky birds rapidly, the river has not been blocked or slowed. There has been nothing more than a mere splash on the surface of our minds. Such disturbances happen to everyone and are in no way sins.

However, inviting the birds down and coaxing them out of the sky is a different story. If we allow those visiting birds to sit on the water and let them dip deeper and deeper in the river for bigger and bigger fish, then the birds will ultimately create a dam, so to speak, in our river. Our progress will be slowed and diverted. Such blockage indicates a sin that requires repentance.

We read in the scriptures that the disobedient "shall be damned" (D&C 42:60). Now and then someone will even quote one such forceful passage over the pulpit (much to the delight of all the snickering deacons in the front two rows at the side of the chapel). We hear the word *damned,* which means "condemned," but doctrinally it translates also into the meaning of the similar word *dammed,* which signifies "stopped up" and "blocked." This is a literal, accurate description of the effect sin has in our lives. Sin blocks our progress. It most literally dams us, keeps us from moving forward in the course God wills us to follow.

So, are my thoughts sins? I can check myself by asking: "Are these thoughts blocking my progress? Are they keeping me from my worthy goals? Are they slowing me in any way?" If the honest answer is yes, then, my thoughts have become sins because I have allowed them to sink below the surface of my mind into my heart. If I do not repent and change, then I am, most definitely, "damned."

My friend Clark Smith says, "You might not be able to keep a bird from landing on your head but you *can* keep him from building a nest there!" Perhaps we can say that we might not be able to keep a bird from landing on our river ("Whosoever *looketh* on a woman") but we *can* keep him from building a multimillion-dollar hydroelectric dam ("to *lust* after her") (Matthew 5:28).

My new friend had only one question more: "Since I can't really stop the birds from landing, how do I get rid of them quickly? How do I control unworthy thoughts?" Elder Robert E. Wells has written, "Self-control will lead to Christ, but that means giving up the things of the world and changing our thoughts" (*The Mount and the Master* [Salt Lake City: Deseret Book Company, 1991], xiii). Brigham Young said, "The greatest mystery a man ever learned is to know how to control the human mind" (*Journal of Discourses,* 1:46).

Following are some of the ideas I shared with my friend. Perhaps one or two might be helpful for you as well.

Replace wrong thoughts with right ones. Most of us have heard that we should sing a hymn when we have evil thoughts. The only problem I've ever had with this advice is that I like to sing. I'll burst out in song just for fun, and you would be amazed at the astonished looks I get from those around me who are sure I need to reread *The Miracle of Forgiveness.*

I remember an occasion during my mission in Chile when my companion and I had to walk by a typical South American beach. I told my companion, "Elder, sing a hymn!" He obediently started singing, "There is beauty all around."

One young woman went to her bishop about the problem of inappropriate thoughts. He said, "Think of a hymn." She responded: "But, Bishop, that's the problem. I can't *stop* thinking of *him.*"

Elder Boyd K. Packer's principle is sound: We get rid of unworthy thoughts by replacing them with worthy ones. As with digging a hole in the backyard, if I don't want the dirt to just get pushed back in when the next rainstorm comes, I had better put something else—like cement—in place of the dirt.

Remove stumbling blocks. We're all familiar with the advice given in Matthew 5:30—"If thy right hand offend thee, cut it off"—yet too many are unclear as to what it really means. Todd Parker teaches: "A better definition of the word *offend* from the original Greek is 'cause to stumble.' In other words, if your . . . hand is tempted to touch something that would cause you to stumble spiritually, the Savior's advice is to get rid of the temptation. You should get away from it or not get near whatever it is that tempts you. He is suggesting that not only do we *not* do the sin, but also that we not even get near the temptation, let alone the sin" (*High Fives and High Hopes* [Salt Lake City: Deseret Book Co., 1990], 96).

Working on Sunday, swearing, listening to inappropriate music, viewing pornography, seeing R-rated movies—*any* R-rated movies—hanging around with friends who are bad influences, dating before sixteen and then pairing up and steady dating having reached sixteen—these are all activities that can feed inappropriate thought birds. Let's do as we are counseled by the Savior and cut out of our lives any activities that are causing us to stumble.

Change environments. Sometimes, when we find ourselves in

places where lights are low and thoughts are even lower, we must simply get out. Change environments. Just as sure as Joseph of old did (see Genesis 39:12), sometimes we just have to run away.

At Especially for Youth a young man came up to me and said, "Brother Wilcox, I know exactly what you mean!" It seems that a certain young lady in his home ward came over to his house to listen to music. His stereo happened to be downstairs in his bedroom, and as they sat on his bed listening, the girl said, "Turn over and I'll give you a back rub."

This young man said to me, "I knew I really shouldn't, but, Brother Wilcox—it felt so good."

After a while, the girl said, "Take off your shirt and I'll rub you with some lotion."

"I knew I shouldn't," came the response again, "but, Brother Wilcox . . ." Suddenly, the girl started taking off *her* shirt. The boy told me: "I didn't know what to do. I didn't want to look stupid, and I didn't want her to think I was weird, but I just said, 'Hey, you want to listen to music? You listen to the music. I'm getting out of here!'" And he ran. Bless him—he ran out of his own house.

Do something active. We are all well aware of the connection between our brains and our bodies. We can all name people who simply could not talk if their hands were tied behind them. However, we do not use this interconnection to our advantage as often as we should. Just as the mind can affect body movement, body movement can affect the mind.

Most of you can remember talking with someone (or speaking at the pulpit in sacrament meeting) when suddenly your mind went completely blank. You were right in the middle of a sentence, but then you could no more remember what you had just been thinking than you could quote 2 Nephi by heart.

When your mind goes blank like that, chances are you have moved your body. That simple movement totally erased a thought. So when we *want* our minds to go blank, let's move.

"Oh, sure," some might be thinking, "jumping jacks in the middle of biology class." Not necessarily. Just try crossing arms, legs, ankles, fingers, and then uncross them and do it again. Move your hands. Wiggle your toes. It sounds strange, but when someone asks you what on earth you're doing you might not remember, and that's the whole idea.

Do "all that stuff." My second-grade daughter calls it "all that stuff." We were having family night and I asked, "What can we do to be happy?" After a long pause, she exhaled loudly, rolled her eyes dramatically, and sighed. "Just . . . just do . . . all that stuff!" The more I think about it, she's absolutely right.

By "all that stuff," she meant to pray; read the scriptures, the *New Era,* and Church books; participate in Young Men or Young Women activities and service projects; attend Church meetings; get close to leaders; request regular interviews with your bishop; fellowship those who are less active; be trustworthy, loyal, helpful, friendly, courteous, kind. . . . The list of constructive activities with which to occupy our minds and our time is endless.

One recently baptized young man was asked whether joining the Church had solved all his problems. He smiled: "No, but it has left me with a lot less time to worry about them." When we're dealing with the problem of unworthy thoughts, we need to remember that the less time we give Satan the less trouble he will be able to give us. "Commit thy works unto the Lord," we are instructed, "and thy thoughts shall be established" (Proverbs 16:3).

Celebrate private victories. When you mow the lawn or do homework, people say, "Wonderful!" If you lose twenty pounds, people say, "Outstanding!" When you get your Duty to God or Young Womanhood Recognition, everyone says, "Excellent!" When I'm really trying to go the extra mile, John Bytheway even says to me, "Thou art cool!"

But what happens when we control our thoughts? Do parents say, "Sweetheart, we know that myriad triple X-rated grossities and impurities are spawning in your mind and you're controlling them. We are so proud of you!" No way! There is no space on the school report card for an A+ in thought control. When I cast out an improper thought, no one really knows except God and me. So it is up to the two of us to throw the party!

Once I was waiting for a plane in an airport in southern California. I was just sitting there writing in my journal when suddenly a man came over, sat down right next to me, and proceeded to unfold a magazine in plain view—and it was *not* the *Ensign!*

I buried my head in my journal. My writing started looking shaky. The sentences were going all over the page, but I just kept writing: "I will not look up. I will not even think about looking up. I will absolutely, definitely not look up."

Now I open my journal to that particular page with a lot of laughs and a great deal of personal pride. It was a victory—a private victory but nonetheless a victory. I celebrated as if my school had just taken state! I praised myself and rewarded myself. I remember the peace that Heavenly Father sent on that occasion—the peace that is promised in Mosiah 4. I felt it. I loved it. I let it reinforce me, and it encouraged me to make the same positive choice again in the future. I was better for having taken a moment to celebrate my private victory.

Be with others. Stay with groups. Be with good friends. Include family. Many young people tell me that when they are at Especially for Youth, a youth conference, or seminary they never have problems with their thoughts. Why? Besides being positive spiritual environments, these activities also involve groups of people. A mind that is focused on others has a hard time focusing on selfish desires. Staying with other people keeps you from being alone with your thoughts.

Obviously, there are times when we have to be alone. We can't bring everyone at EFY over to watch us go to sleep every night or get ready in the morning. If those are times when unworthy thoughts creep in, leave your bedroom door ajar or the bathroom door unlocked. That small effort to open yourself to others will leave you feeling much less secure and comfortable in personal moments. Believe me, the fact that someone else could, might, and probably will come in at any time is enough to keep you on track. Knowing that you could at any minute be entertaining a little brother or sister might just be enough to keep you from entertaining temptation.

Understand dreams. Perhaps dreams are the most misunderstood realm of thought. Now and then, most of us feel a little shocked by what we dream. On those mornings, the best thing to do is simply let it go. Forget the dream and move on.

Our dreams are classical, respondent behavior, controlled completely by preceding stimuli—much like the constriction of the pupils of our eyes when someone shines a flashlight at them. Given the bright light, we cannot consciously will our pupils not to constrict. In the same way, we cannot consciously control our dreams, and thus we cannot be held accountable for them and should not feel so bad about them. Let dreams go. It's okay to leave the night behind and begin the day in peace.

If dreams become a major problem, rather than focusing on what is coming out of your mind at night, zero in on what is being allowed into your mind during the day—especially right before bed. If I don't want constricted pupils, I'd better not let anyone with a flashlight even close to my eyes.

Remember the Savior. All of us have made covenants to remember Christ always (see D&C 20:77, 79). What better time to remember him than when we are having unworthy thoughts? Truman G. Madsen suggests: "Picture Christ and remember how you are bound to him. In the crisis, for example, when your temples thunder, imagine what you are tempted to do as if it were a large sledge hammer. See! See if you can stand at the cross and by this act of indulgence swing that hammer on the nail. That will break your compulsive pattern and restore enough to your consciousness to enable you to cry out and *mean*, 'No!'" (*Christ and the Inner Life,* 37).

In the Doctrine and Covenants, the Lord tells us, "Look unto me in every thought" (6:36). Elder Robert E. Wells teaches that the true key to becoming a disciple of Christ is to fill your mind with thoughts of the Savior, fill your heart with love of the Savior, and fill your life with service. "Through following these paths," writes Elder Wells, "bad men become good and good men become better; the sinner becomes a saint" (*We Are Christians Because . . .* [Salt Lake City: Deseret Book Co., 1985], 108).

Request a special blessing. Ask for a blessing from your father or a priesthood leader. Just as Christ blessed eyes to see and ears to hear, I believe that minds can be blessed to think on higher levels.

"Oh sure," some might say. "I'm going to just run up to my dad and ask him to bless me to get my brain out of the gutter." Dads and priesthood leaders understand much more than we might think they will. However, if you feel uncomfortable, you do not need to tell anyone the specific reason why you are requesting a blessing, for a sensitive priesthood holder will simply take his place as a mouthpiece. You will receive your special blessing and counsel from our all-seeing Heavenly Father, who understands completely, in the name of Jesus Christ, who knows exactly how you feel—not in some mythical Santa-knows-whether-you-have-been-naughty-or-nice way, but rather because he has been there.

"Are any of our conceivable evil thoughts beyond the Lord? If so, would there be any sound foundation for trust in him? . . .

". . . How low then can we go in our thoughts? Not as low as he in the contemplation of evil. He was tempted through 'The darkest abyss' and 'descended below all things.' Why? That he might be 'in and through *all* things the light of truth.' What? In and through *my* vagrant, aching, turbulent, unworthy thoughts? 'Yes. . . .' He has comprehended them all. His is the compassion of kinship. (D&C 88:6)" (Truman G. Madsen, *Christ and the Inner Life,* 34–35).

Think it through to the end. After we have tried to cast out evil thoughts and they still linger, perhaps we need to try a different approach. Rather than thinking so hard about not thinking, try instead taking the time to think—really think. And, more important, think beyond.

If I take time to analyze each little detail of a passionate fantasy, I must also take time to think of the other moments that are sure to follow—not fantasies at all. I must think of the guilt that will be felt by my spirit as surely as pain is felt by my body. I must picture having to face people the following day and imagine looking in my own mirror. I must ponder about having to tell parents and a bishop. Further, I must think thirty years down the road, when I'll be bringing my children to Temple Square for general conference and there maybe running into a certain person from the past who is also visiting. How will I feel when I end up in a situation in which I might actually have to introduce my children to that person?

Everyone loves fireworks on the Fourth of July, but few consider that on the fifth of July someone has to clean up the mess. Elder M. Russell Ballard explains: "One of Satan's clever tactics is to tempt us to concentrate on the present and ignore the future. . . . We must govern our actions every day with our future in mind" (*Ensign,* November 1990, 36).

Keep perspective. "The Lord gives us the feelings of love and attraction, strong bonds that he wants us to use as the center of a united, eternal family. What you must do is learn to channel those feelings in the right direction, to understand them as part of the process of growing and learning, of preparing for a temple marriage, leading someday to family life in a celestial realm" (*New Era,* May 1989, 18).

Many of the same thoughts that are carelessly referred to as "bad" will someday, in the right place, at the right time, with the right person, be very good. Remember, passions are not meant to be eliminated, expelled, and cut out of our lives forever. They are to be bridled (see Alma 38:12). Appetites are not to be removed but to be regulated. Desires are not to be ruled out but to be ruled. Thoughts are not to be conquered but to be controlled.

"It's my thoughts." That's what my dark-haired friend said to me after the fireside. "Sometimes I just have the worst thoughts." I hope he now knows that he is not alone. I hope he knows that lots of people understand and care. Most of all, I hope he knows that he can control unworthy thoughts. We all can. It is important. It is possible. With Heavenly Father's help, all of us can "let virtue garnish [our] thoughts unceasingly" so that our "confidence [will] wax strong in the presence of God" (D&C 121:45).

Brad Wilcox grew up in Provo, Utah, except for childhood years spent in Ethiopia, Africa. He served a mission in Chile and is now married and has four children. He received a Ph.D. in education from the University of Wyoming in 1994. Brad is an associate professor in the Department of Teacher Education at Brigham Young University. He has served as the bishop of a BYU ward and lived with his family in New Zealand, where he directed a study abroad program. He currently serves as a full-time mission president.

8

I JUST WANT TO BE HAPPY

Barbara Barrington Jones

Recently I received a letter from a young woman in which she said, "I would like to ask you something if I could. I know you're not a counselor or anything, but I was wondering how I could feel better about myself, feel more accepted by my peers, and be more happy all the time." She went on to say, "I dread getting up every morning to go to school. My sister and I have not been getting along either. She's seventeen, and I'm sixteen. She has a boyfriend and is very pretty. She's skinny and used to be a model. I'm nothing like that. So I think I'm a little jealous."

Before I tell you how I answered her letter, let's back up a little bit and talk about feeling good about ourselves.

When we're born, we have 100 percent self-esteem. Considering where we just came from, why would we have any less? Then things start to change. By the time we get into grade school, here are the statistics: 67 percent of the guys still feel good about themselves; 60 percent of the girls feel positive about themselves.

In high school, 49 percent of the boys feel good about themselves. That means over half don't feel good about themselves.

And just 24 percent of the girls feel good. (Statistics provided by *The American Association of University Women.)*

Why?

Why do we lose our self-esteem? Why do we lose our capacity to be happy? Why do we become blind to our real potential?

My husband cut an article out of "Dear Abby" for me. The headline was "Don't Judge a Gift By Its Cover." The letter told this story:

> A young man from a wealthy family was about to graduate from high school. It was the custom in that affluent neighborhood for the parents to give the graduate an automobile. "Bill" and his father had spent months looking at cars, and the week before graduation they found the perfect car. Bill was certain the car would be his on graduation night.
>
> Imagine his disappointment when, on the eve of his graduation, Bill's father handed him a gift-wrapped Bible! Bill was so angry that he threw the Bible down and stormed out of the house. He and his father never saw each other again. It was the news of his father's death that finally brought Bill home.
>
> As he sat one night going through his father's possessions that he was to inherit, he came across the Bible his father had given him. He brushed away the dust and opened it to find a cashier's check, dated the day of his graduation, in the exact amount of the price of the car they had chosen together.

As you read this, I believe your reaction will be much like mine. I said to myself, "Stupid, stupid guy. Why didn't you just open your gift? Didn't you know that in this book there is everything you could ever want? Not only would you have had the material thing you wanted—the car—but you would have had an instruction manual on how to live this life and how to be happy." He was too quick to judge the gift that was given him.

What can we learn from this story?

We came to earth with everything: 100 percent self-esteem and countless gifts from Heavenly Father. But we have to search for our gifts. We have to open each gift and make the most of it. We all have gifts, but what makes me so sad is that so many times we don't recognize them because we spend so much time comparing ourselves to others.

This is a portion of a letter I received from a girl. She wrote:

I feel so inadequate, so inferior, so average. I watch and study everyone around me—people, pictures in magazines, actresses, everyone—picking out every feature that I wish I could have for myself. In every person I see a trait that I rip myself apart for not having or for not being able to do as well. Jealousy has made me a depressed and hopeless person.

I'll go through everything, one thing at a time. I'm overweight and have been forever. Furthermore, I make goals continually and fail every time. I am absolutely totally grotesque.

My hair's a mess—permed, colored, no shine. It's not romantically long, or curly or short, or stylish—it's nothing.

My eyebrows are each different. They have no shape or curved line. They droop and the hair grows in all directions.

My eyelashes grow every direction and cannot be straightened or curled. They are also not long, dark, curly, or full.

My nose is long, even my mother would admit, because she has the same one, only not quite as bad.

My face is round and chubby. My skin is splotched. My teeth are straight but very yellowish in color because of another one of my revolting, self-destructive, spiritually killing, socially repulsive habits—bulimia.

She went on to list every part of herself she disliked, right down to her toes. Do you see what she's doing? Every day she's looking in that mirror and picking herself apart. It is not constructive criticism. She's destroying herself by overlooking the good things about herself. But this isn't going on just with young women.

I met a young man in Dallas at a youth conference. His parents later flew him to my house to go through my seminar because his self-esteem was so low. His name is Paul Anderson.

When I first met him, he was slim, not too tall, and couldn't look you in the face. In trying to get to know him, I asked, "What do you like to do? Do you like to play sports?"

He said, "No, I hate sports."

"How about school? Do you like school?"

"No, not really."

My husband and I spent one solid week trying to get him to say something he liked to do, trying to get him to open the cover and take his gift out of the box. He wouldn't do it.

Finally, at the end of the week, I asked him, "What do you do when you get home from school?"

He said, "Play the piano."

"Oh, you play the piano?"

"Yeah. Do you want to see pictures of my family?"

The first picture he pulled out of his wallet was of his brother— a total jock—captain of the football team, blond crew cut, and a muscular build.

What had my friend been doing? He had been comparing himself with his brother. He acted as if his piano playing were unimportant or insignificant.

I asked, "What kind of things do you play on the piano after school?"

He went into my living room, sat down at the piano, and, with an attitude of who cares anyway? said, "Well, I wrote this."

He started playing this beautiful piece of music that he had composed.

I couldn't believe it. He was totally ignoring his own gifts because he was so busy judging himself by the outside—the cover. And his cover wasn't like his brother's.

He worked on overcoming his negative attitude about himself. He eventually served a mission, then, after he returned, he sent me the cover of his first album. With a great-looking photo of himself on the front, it was entitled, "Paul Anderson, Himself." He had written: "To Sister Jones, who has given me so much. I love you tons.

Paul." He had unwrapped his gift and made it available for the whole world to enjoy.

All he had to do was open the gift.

Do you base how you feel on how you perform? Do you base how you feel about yourself on what other people say? Do you base how you feel about yourself on your physical appearance?

You have so many gifts that are untouched. But you have to do your part. Heavenly Father is not going to do it for you. You have to take the gift out. You have to search for it. God judges from the inside.

The greatest thing that you can do for your self-esteem is to come to know the Savior. As I was teaching a class the other day, a bishop walked up to the front of the room, right in the middle of the class. He asked, "May I say something?"

I handed the microphone to him. This is the story he told:

When I was eight years old, I was really into baseball. I had every player's baseball card. My dad saved his money to send me to a baseball camp run by a star player.

The first day the famous guy running the camp, who was kind of cocky, had the list of names. My name is spelled S-t-e-p-h-e-n. He looked at the list and asked, "Where's old Stephan?" He purposely mispronounced my name.

I cringed as everyone started to laugh.

The coach continued to call, "Step-han, are you here? Hey, Step-han."

I felt worse and worse. Everyone was laughing harder and harder. It was the worst experience of my life. When I got home, I told my dad I would never play baseball again.

My dad was a wise man and waited a few years. Then a retired player came to town and started a Little League program. Dad took the new coach aside and said, "My son loves baseball so much. But he had a bad experience with a coach." And he told the coach the whole story.

The new coach said, "You send him to me for tryouts."

I barely made the team but improved as the season progressed. Then the time came when it was a win or lose situation for my team. The bases were loaded. It was my turn at bat. I thought the coach was going to bring in a pinch hitter for me. But the coach didn't. He walked over and put his arm around me and said, "Stephen, you can do it. I'm your coach. I'm behind you all the way. You can do it."

I walked up to the plate. I did not hit the ball out of the ballpark. But I did hit a fly to the center fielder that was deep enough to allow the runner from third to tag up and beat the throw to home. Our team won the game.

Stephen's coach had faith in him. The bishop continued his story:

I'll never forget that coach. Then I grew up and got another coach in my life. My new coach came to me one night and said, "Stephen, you're going on a mission." And when I said to him, "I don't think I can do it," he said, "I have faith in you. I know you can do it." My new coach was Jesus Christ.

I went on a mission. Then my coach came to me again one night, after I had gotten married, and said, "Stephen, you're going to be in charge of the Blazer Bs."

I said, "Coach, I can't be in charge of them."

The Savior said, "Yes, you can. I have faith in you."

And then this newly called, young bishop, with emotion choking him, said, "He came to me two months ago and said, 'Stephen, you're going to be the bishop.'"

And Stephen said, "I can't be the bishop."

The Savior said, "I'll be right beside you every step of the way."

This man learned to listen to the One who knew his potential and who would support him.

The only way you'll be happy, the only way you'll feel good about yourself, is to get a new *coach*. Listen to someone who knows and loves the real you. Make the Savior Jesus Christ your *coach.*

That's the most important piece of advice I can give you.

I would like to close with a true story about an immigrant girl who, at the age of fifteen, just ached inside because she was so unhappy. Coming from a foreign country, she felt that she would never be accepted or ever have friends. During the two years she had been attending high school since arriving in the United States from Germany, she had seldom spoken to any of the other students. She never felt as though she fit in. She was self-conscious about her accent, her hand-me-down clothes, her long, thick braids, and even her lunches of dark rye bread that her mother packed for her each day.

One day as she sat in the library reading a book, she looked outside through the window at two girls who were sitting on the lawn. They were laughing and talking together. She could tell they were best friends. *Oh, I just wish I could have a friend, even one friend, that I could talk with,* she thought.

When she got home, she went to her room, sat on the edge of her bed, put her face in her hands, and cried. As the tears streamed down her cheeks, she lifted her head, and her gaze fell on a picture of the Savior, hanging on the wall across the room. She thought how friendly his face looked. She had been taught all her life how much he loves and cares for each of us. As she looked at the picture, she whispered, "Jesus, I'm so lonely."

The next day after school one of the girls asked her if she would be going to the school dance that night. She abruptly said, "No!" As she boarded the bus to go home, all she could think of was the last dance she had attended, where she had sat on the sidelines for hours by herself. Finally, a young man had walked up to her, but instead of asking her to dance, he had yanked on one of her braids. Everyone had laughed, and she had been humiliated. No, she would never go to a dance again.

Reaching home, she walked through the stillness of her empty house. Her mother worked every day, and her younger sisters and brother were out playing with their friends. If they had friends, why couldn't she have friends? Was there something wrong with her? She ran to her room and threw herself on the bed. Her body shook with sobs.

She sat up suddenly. Someone was in the room! Quickly, she wiped away her tears so that whoever it was wouldn't know she had been crying. She looked around but saw no one there. There was an undeniable presence and a feeling of overwhelming love like she had never felt before. She knew who it was. "Jesus," she whispered, "is it you?"

He answered, not with a voice that could be heard by human ears, but with a feeling of love so strong that it penetrated her heart. She saw no human form, but with her spirit she saw his smiling face and his eyes that seemed to say, "You are my special friend." And, sitting there on her bed, she seemed to hear his gentle words, "I will never leave you or forsake you. Don't be afraid or ashamed. I love you just the way you are." She had never felt such unconditional love in her life.

For three glorious months that presence stayed with her. He was there when she awoke and when she caught the bus. He stood by her desk in school and ran beside her in gym. She was gloriously happy. Her family couldn't believe it as they observed her smiling and heard her humming as she set the table.

One day at the bus stop, as the usual group of teens gathered, he seemed to say to her, "Aren't these youth great? I love each one of them dearly." She smiled as she began to see her classmates through the Savior's eyes. It wasn't long before they began to include her in their conversations. At last, she was beginning to belong. At last, she felt accepted. At last, she was happy.

She awoke one morning to find the presence gone. She wondered if she had done something wrong. She confessed every sin, but she was still alone. In desperation she picked up her Bible, looking for those special words that he had said to her that first day. She found them in Hebrews 13:5: "For he hath said, I will never leave thee, nor forsake thee."

He said, "never," so that she might know that even though she didn't feel his presence, he was still with her. She seemed to hear him say, "You will find me in my written word, and in the faces of the people you meet, and in many other different ways." She suddenly realized how blessed she had been to have the Savior with her for that very special time in her life. He had taught her that true happiness comes from seeing ourselves and others through his eyes (adapted from Helen Grace Lescheid, *Guideposts,* September 1992).

The Savior will be there as our special friend and our *Coach.* If we follow his perfect example to love others as he loves us, we will find true happiness.

Barbarra Barrington Jones is an international image consultant, author, lecturer, fashion designer, former classical ballet dancer and actress, and professional model. A director of summer youth programs at BYU, Sister Jones also grooms young women for competition in national and international beauty pageants. She enjoys walking, preparing and eating healthy foods, and working with youth. Barbara and her husband, Hal, reside in Novato, California, and they have two children.

9

GET OFF THE BENCH!
Matthew O. Richardson

A few years ago, my son wanted a football uniform for Christmas. I'm sure that you know the type: a plastic helmet bearing your favorite team's insignia, an "official" jersey, miniature shoulder pads, and a pair of nylon pants that are either way too short or four sizes too large. (Zach's were too large!) On Christmas morning, Zachary found his package under the tree and frantically clawed the paper away to reveal his coveted football uniform. I still remember the jubilant smile he wore while pumping his arm in the air and saying, "Yes! Santa loves me!" My wife and I smiled and winked at each other. Zach didn't waste any time putting that uniform on. As soon as it was on, he charged throughout the house "scoring touchdowns" and "blocking" his little sister. (We later had to make that a penalty—illegal block to the sister.) I remember hearing a little growl, like an engine running, and I would look down to find Zachary clinging to my leg. "What are you doing?" I would ask. "I'm tackling you, Dad!"

Zachary loved his little uniform. He wore it all day long. When it came time to eat dinner, Zachary sat at the table with his helmet strapped securely to his head. We asked him to take it off, but he quickly informed us that "real football players eat with their helmets on." Since it was Christmas, we thought it wouldn't hurt to let him try. Besides, it was funny watching him try to guide the spoon through the face mask to his mouth. Zachary slept in that football uniform, because, after all, "real football players sleep in their uniforms." Needless to say, Zachary wore that uniform for days. I was worried that maybe he was too much into the uniform thing. My wife chuckled and said that she thought I was probably just like that when I was a kid. Although I denied it, she was absolutely right. I couldn't wait to get a uniform when I was Zach's age.

I remember as a kid looking through my older brother's high school yearbook and finding the sports section. I longingly looked at the teams in their uniforms and yearned to be part of them. As I flipped through the pages, I came across a section that had "Mighty Men, Model Men, Murray [the name of my high school] Men" written in bold letters across the top. That sounded so cool, I had to read it again. "Mighty Men, Model Men, Murray Men." Below this title were pictures of young men all wearing the same type of jacket. I recognized some of them from the team pictures on the previous pages, but not everyone in the team picture was in this "Mighty Man" section . . . only some. I learned later that this was the "Letterman's Club" picture. Right then and there, I decided that I wanted to be a letterman. I didn't have the slightest idea what a letterman was, but I wanted to be one.

I later found out that the letterperson designation wasn't exclusive to sports but included members of clubs, the choir, student government, academics, and other groups. When it came to letterpersons, however, it wasn't enough to simply be part of the organization, wear their uniform, or go to their meetings. According to standards at my high school, a letterperson had to "make a significant contribution to the success of the organization." In other words, a letterperson was a necessary part of the organization—one that the organization couldn't do without.

With today's challenges, we have need of more letterpersons in life. That's right, life! As a matter of fact, even our prophets have talked about life in terms of a game. President Ezra Taft Benson once said: "You are a royal generation. The heavenly grandstands are cheering you on. The Lord is our coach and manager. His team will win and we can be a valiant part of it if we so desire. Rise up, O youth of Zion! You hardly realize the great divine potential that lies within you" ("In His Steps," in *Speeches of the Year* 1979 [Provo: Brigham Young University Press, 1980], 59).

Just think: you are part of that unique team—the team of Jesus Christ. You joined his team when you were baptized, and you put on his uniform as you took his name upon you. It has been written that "your generation will fight the greatest army of Satanic hosts ever assembled" (*Church News,* May 9, 1991). As we face such stern opposition, we will need every member of the team to "make a significant contribution." We don't just need more members, we need more letterpersons for Christ. Therefore, how are you treating your uniform of Christ? You are wearing it, aren't you?

John the Beloved had a warning for those who would wear Christ's uniform in the latter days. Speaking through John, the Lord said, "I know thy works, that thou art neither cold nor hot: I would thou wert cold or hot. So then because thou art lukewarm, and neither cold nor hot, I will spue thee out of my mouth" (Revelation 3:15–16). John is pleading with us to stand up, make a difference, be identified with the uniform of Christ that we are wearing. We live in a time when we can't sit on the back row, halfheartedly living the gospel standards. We need to turn up the temperature, make our contribution. So how does someone become a letterperson for Jesus Christ? How do we make a significant contribution to the success of the Church and the gospel of Christ? May I suggest three ideas for your consideration.

Stand Up for Your Team!

Something special happens when we learn to stand up for . . . almost anything. Power comes from loyalty and devotion. For example, I remember playing tennis with two of my older brothers and my older sister at a park near my home. Playing tennis on the court next to ours were two boys, the same age as my sister. While they were playing, they said something about my sister that was rude. My sister, a very sensitive person, heard what they said and started to cry. I was trying to comfort her when I heard a loud clang. It came from the gate between the two tennis courts as it banged shut after my brothers ran through it. You see, these boys made the comment loudly enough that not just my sister but my older brothers heard it as well. By the time I raced through the gate and onto the other court, my older brothers had already captured their prey. One of my brothers was sitting on the chest of one young man, and my other brother had his prey pinned against the fence. I remember my brothers saying, "Nobody says anything like that about my sister . . . nobody!" I must confess I was confused because I was thinking to myself, "Wait a minute, you said that very thing to her just last night!" But something important was happening. When push came to shove, I learned that as brothers and sisters, we stood up for each other. If you are going to fight one Richardson, you will have to fight us all.

It is one thing to stand up for your family, but it is equally important to stand up for the gospel. In actuality it isn't that much different, and it can happen in a variety of ways. I used to ride the bus to school. I remember arriving at the bus stop one day and finding the other students huddled together in a group. As I approached, one of my friends popped his head up out of the huddle, and he shouted anxiously at me to "hurry up." As I got closer, other friends began yelling to me, "Come on, Matt. Hurry up." Then I heard them saying, "You just wait. Matt will show you—you just wait!"

"Hi, guys!" I said cheerily, sensing that something was up.

"Show him, Matt. You just tell him!"

"Tell who . . . what?" I asked. There in the middle of the group was Ronnie, the neighborhood anti-Mormon. He had told my friends that Mormon kids were nothing more than a bunch of sheep, that we didn't know the first thing about our church, and that we just followed our parents around, doing whatever they said. Bless my friends' hearts, they had stood up to Ronnie. "No, we're not," they had said confidently, "we're not sheep!"

"Prove it," Ronnie shot back. "Tell me one thing about your church."

My friends were really confident now. "Okay, Ronnie," they said, "you just wait till Matt Richardson gets here; he'll tell you all about our church." There I stood—shocked.

"Come on, Mormon," Ronnie smirked, "one thing."

My mind went blank. The only thing I could think of about the Church was refreshments and church basketball, and neither one of those seemed to be what was needed. Luckily, the bus came and we got on. "Saved by the bus!" I thought.

Ronnie didn't let up, however. "Come on, Mormon, one thing," he repeated, and then he started making sheep calls. I was so frustrated. I remember saying a *real* prayer in my heart. Ronnie was relentless. And then it hit me. I sat up straight and looked Ronnie square in the eyes. "Ronnie," I started. "We believe in God the Eternal Father, and in His Son, Jesus Christ, and in the Holy Ghost." I just kept on going. "We believe that men will be punished for their own sins . . ." I didn't stop until I had recited all thirteen Articles of Faith. There was a purpose for Primary after all!

I wish that I could tell you that we stopped by the local swimming pool on the way to school to baptize Ronnie, but it didn't happen that way. As a matter of fact, I don't know what ever happened to Ronnie. He moved from our neighborhood shortly after that experience, and I haven't seen or heard from him since. Although Ronnie didn't get off the bus a different person, there was somebody who did—me! I knew that what I had told Ronnie was true. I realized that I knew more about the gospel of Jesus Christ than I thought I did and, even more important, I had stood up for my team.

Maybe this is what Paul meant as he boldly declared that he was ready to teach the gospel, even in Rome (where his life would be taken). He was a prime example of one who stood up for Christ's gospel, for Paul was "not ashamed of the gospel of Christ" (Romans 1:16). This same attitude was reflected in the early Apostles who were commanded by the Sanhedrin council "not to speak at all nor teach in the name of Jesus" (Acts 4:18). But the Apostles were always found teaching thereafter in the name of Christ. The council arrested them again and threatened them, scolded them, and on occasion even beat them. "Did not we straitly command you that ye should not teach in [Jesus'] name?" a frustrated and wicked council member inquired of the Apostles (Acts 5:28). Undaunted, Peter and the other Apostles answered, "We ought to obey God rather than men" (Acts 5:29). Stand up, O youth of Zion!

Keep Your Uniform On at All Times

One of the keys to the success of any team or organization is to always know who is on your side. You can imagine how disastrous it would be if someone from the opposing team posed as a fellow team member, or if one of your team members decided to change to the opposing team in the middle of the game. Think how confusing and frustrating it would be if you had some members of either team wearing half of your uniform and half of the other team's uniform. In a way, a uniform tells you who you can trust and who you can't.

In order to make a significant contribution to Christ's team, his players must keep their uniforms on at all times. Christ's players cannot afford to take off any part of his uniform, even for just a moment. Perhaps this is what Alma was emphasizing when he admonished us to "stand as witnesses of God at all times and in all things, and in all places that ye may be in" (Mosiah 18:9). In a way, that is exactly what we promise each time we partake of the sacrament. To those members who faithfully wear the uniform of Christ at all times, in all things, in every place, and under all circumstances, come significant understanding, comfort, and blessings. Paul wrote to a group of Saints who were struggling with this very problem (standing up for the gospel) and encouraged them to "be zealously affected always in a good thing, and not only when I am present with you" (Galatians 4:18). A good question may be, How does becoming a letterperson for Christ relate to Paul's invitation to "be zealously affected"? Perhaps this example will help answer that question.

During my senior year in high school, my car would run out of gas on a regular basis. On one occasion, I remember putting gasoline in my car only to find that it still wouldn't start. My best friend and I quickly discovered that my fuel line was blocked and that gasoline wasn't getting to the engine. I remembered my father once telling me an experience from his younger days, when he had had a similar problem. He filled a soda pop bottle with gasoline and poured the gasoline straight into the carburetor, thus bypassing the fuel line altogether.

I relayed this story to my best friend, and we decided to try my dad's old trick. We filled a large paint can with gas and walked from the gas station back to my car. By the time we arrived it was dark and the street was only dimly lit by a single street lamp on the corner. We raised the hood and uncovered the carburetor, and then I jumped into the driver's seat.

With the hood raised, my vision of what was happening was obstructed except through a small space between the raised hood and the bottom of the windshield. I could barely see Kurt's hands and part of the gasoline-filled paint can through the small gap. I watched as Kurt carefully tipped the can and poured gasoline into the carburetor.

"Hit it!" Kurt yelled. I quickly turned the key and heard the whirling grind, but the car still didn't start. As soon as I turned the key off, I could see Kurt pour more gas into the open carburetor.

"Try it again!" he yelled. I turned the key and pumped the gas pedal with the same results—nothing.

"I don't think this will work," I yelled to Kurt.

"Third time's a charm," Kurt hollered back as he poured some more gas into the carburetor. "Try it again!" I turned the key but, unlike the times before, the engine cranked over only once. Then there was a loud bang, and a bright flash of light darted through the hood's gap where I was watching. I couldn't remember anything about bangs and flashes from my dad's story.

What followed next was something that I will never forget. I looked out of the passenger window and saw my best friend engulfed in flames from his knees to his head. He literally lit up the dark night as he whirled around in circles, frantically slapping at the flames. I remember how everything happened so fast . . . but at the same time so slowly. I realized that I was screaming in my mind: *Stop! Drop! Roll!* But Kurt wasn't stopping, he wasn't dropping, and he definitely wasn't rolling!

The next thing I remember was sitting on Kurt's chest, slapping his head with my hands, trying to put the flames out. I had gotten out of the car, chased him down, tackled him, and now I was so scared that I was trying hard not to cry as I was extinguishing the flames. I suddenly realized that Kurt was no longer on fire, but I was still slapping him. I also realized that now I was really screaming at him. "Why didn't you stop, drop, and roll?" Kurt was trying to answer, which is actually quite difficult to do with someone sitting on your chest and slapping your face and head like a deranged madman. "I was trying to," Kurt would say between slaps.

After I came to my senses and realized that Kurt was no longer on fire, I hurried to take care of my car, which was also burning. As soon as everything was under control, I returned to Kurt and asked, "Why didn't you stop, drop, and roll?" He simply replied that he had wanted to save his baseball jacket.

I have thought about that experience many times over the intervening years. I hope we would never put our lives at risk over any thing, but I have thought about the power of Kurt's determination to save his jacket in light of Paul's admonition to the Saints in Galatia regarding being "zealously affected." Just think if we, as members of Christ's team, were empowered with Kurt's zeal to save and keep the uniform of Christ on at all times. With such determination, we wouldn't remove the uniform of Christ, even at the peril of our own life.

This reminds me of Paul, as he taught the Saints in his letter to the Ephesians to "take unto you the whole armour of God, that ye may be able to withstand in the evil day, and having done all, to stand"

(Ephesians 6:13). Do we really think that we can go into the battles of life having left part of our armor at home and still escape unscathed? Can we take off part of our armor during a party, on a date, while watching certain videos, or in almost anything we do without the opposition exploiting our weakness? Don't you think that the enemy would easily recognize a missing piece of an opponent's armor? Do you honestly believe that if a soldier was found without his breast-plate during a battle, the enemy would incessantly pound away on his helmet (or some other protected area) and not strike at the exposed chest? Not likely. We must follow Paul's advice to wear *all* of the uniform of Christ's team—at all times.

Wear Your Uniform with Honor and Dignity

Finally, we realize there is a great, even unique, strength that is enjoyed by members of a team who represent their team or organization with honor and dignity. I used to treat my sports uniforms with special care. I guess they were special because they were more than fabric. They represented my city, my school, my classmates, and my fellow teammates. I remember watching my wife as a bride, dressed in her wedding dress, walk with great care so as not to soil her dress. But even more impressive than her dress was the way she walked. She glowed with confidence, happiness, and a bright vision of her future. Her uniform (dress) surely made her feel beautiful, but at the same time and even more significantly, she brought beauty to her dress.

In a similar yet far more meaningful way, I think of a pair of gloves my wife has that she treats with great respect. I remember the first time that she showed me her gloves. She took them out carefully and displayed them with great pride. By the way she was behaving, I figured that these gloves must be made of silk or that they were antiques—something had to be special about these gloves, judging by the way she treated them. To my surprise, they were simple, white cotton gloves, not really that *special* at all. But then my wife told me their history. "The last time I wore these gloves, I was eight years old. These are the gloves that I wore when I shook the hand of President Spencer W. Kimball, the prophet of God!" I suddenly realized why they were so important. My wife's reverence for what they represented made them important. They reminded her of the deep love she had for a prophet of God.

My wife's gloves remind me of a similar experience concerning the uniform of Christ. While standing in line to eat dinner as missionaries in the MTC, my companion and I decided to go to the foyer, where pictures of all the Apostles hung, and see if we could name them all by sight. As we were standing in front of their portraits trying to put names with faces, I heard a small, tender voice behind me. Although it was not directed at me, I knew that it was *about* me. I turned around to see a small girl holding hands with her grandmother. "Grandma," she asked, "are those *real* missionaries?" Her little finger was outstretched and pointed directly at me. "Yes, honey," her grandma answered, "those are *real* missionaries!"

To fully understand this experience, you must understand that this little girl didn't simply ask if we were missionaries, she asked if we were *real* missionaries, and the way she asked it made it sound like she was asking her grandma about celebrities or somebody really special. I remember bending over to shake her hand and introduce myself. "My name is Elder Richardson and this is my companion. We have been called to teach the gospel of Christ in Denmark." Then I had to say it. "And yes, we are *real* missionaries!" I felt so special, so empowered, so proud of being a missionary, it was hard to resist singing "High on the Mountain Top" at the top of my lungs.

I will never forget that little girl. She looked at me with such wonder that it made me feel honorable and special. She looked at the uniform of a missionary, complete with the black name tag, as something that was so important, it made me feel important. It was just like my wife's gloves. They were important and special because they were treated in a special way. I felt special as a missionary, at that time, because a small girl treated me like I was special.

I thought often about that experience throughout my mission. Whenever I felt that I was in a compromising situation, the memory of that little girl would come to mind, particularly her little voice: "Grandma, are those *real* missionaries?" I wondered what that little girl would think if she saw me making a wrong choice. How could I disgrace the image she (and I) had of missionaries—*real* missionaries? Would she be proud of the way I was treating my uniform? Bless that little girl's heart, whoever she is, for she helped me wear my uniform as a missionary with greater honor and dignity. The most amazing thing, however, was that as I attempted to wear my uniform of Christ with honor and dignity, honor and dignity came to me.

I believe that we can be a great strength to The Church of Jesus Christ of Latter-day Saints if we stand up for our team, keep our uniform of Christ (all of it) on at all times, and learn to wear it worthily. It is not enough, however, to merely wear the uniform. We live in a time where we must do more, be more. We must strive to become letterpersons—persons who make a significant contribution to the success of the Church. John wrote: "He that saith he abideth in [Christ] ought himself also so to walk, even as he walked" (1 John 2:6).

May we stand united in our efforts to be strong in the gospel. May we be united in being easily identified as Saints. And may we remain faithful in our thoughts, words, and deeds, in all places, at all times, and in all circumstances as we walk as the Master walked, is my humble hope and prayer.

Matthew O. Richardson was born in Salt Lake City, Utah, and served a mission to Denmark. He received a bachelor's degree in communications, a master's degree in educational leadership and curriculum, and a doctorate in educational leadership. Brother Richardson is an associate professor of Church History and Doctrine at Brigham Young University. He has served in various Church callings, including as a bishop, and is currently his ward's mission leader. He and his wife, Lisa, have four children and live in Orem, Utah.

10

RECEIVING THE MIND AND WILL OF THE LORD

Randall C. Bird

Several years ago in a seminary classroom, a student raised his hand and asked, "How can a person say he knows the Church and gospel are true?" Several other students said they had the same question. Seeing that this was important to the students, we embarked on an experience that I will always remember. I had just finished two weeks of in-service training with the Church Educational System. During that training we had discussed some of the principles involved in receiving revelation. How grateful I was for that training. It helped me teach my students the principles governing revelation and testimony. I would like to share with you some of what happened in the classroom that day.

The President of the United States once asked the Prophet Joseph Smith how our religion differed from other religions of that day. Joseph explained that Mormons differed in the way they viewed the gift of the Holy Ghost (see *History of the Church,* 4:42). In other words, revelation by the power of the Holy Ghost is a prime characteristic of the true Church. I find it interesting that the Prophet Joseph answered in such a manner. Often, when a seminary teacher asks LDS students how the Church differs from other churches, students cite such things as: temple marriage, the Word of Wisdom, the concept of three degrees of glory, or some other point of doctrine unique to The Church of Jesus Christ of Latter-day Saints. Why, then, would the Prophet Joseph respond by mentioning the Holy Ghost?

To understand Joseph's answer, I think we must first define revelation. First, revelation is the means by which God communicates intelligence (light and truth) to man. The Lord has said, "The glory of God is intelligence, or, in other words, light and truth" (D&C 93:36). The scriptures also teach that "whatsoever they [the servants of the Lord] shall speak when moved upon by the Holy Ghost shall be scripture, shall be the will of the Lord, shall be the mind of the Lord, shall be the word of the Lord, shall be the voice of the Lord, and the power of God unto salvation" (D&C 68:4).

Next, revelation (light and truth) is communicated in an essentially spirit-to-spirit process, although some of our physical senses may be involved. The Prophet Joseph taught, "All things whatsoever God in his infinite wisdom has seen fit and proper to reveal to us, while we are dwelling in mortality . . . are revealed to us in the abstract, and independent of affinity of this mortal tabernacle, but are revealed to our spirits precisely as though we had no bodies at all; and those revelations which will save our spirits will save our bodies" (*Teachings of the Prophet Joseph Smith*, sel. Joseph Fielding Smith [Salt Lake City: Deseret Book Co., 1976], 355).

Third, revelation is one of the foundation stones the Church is built upon. Peter was once asked by the Savior, "Whom say ye that I am?" He responded by saying, "Thou are the Christ, the Son of the living God." Peter had received a personal revelation of this truth. Jesus then declared "Upon this rock I will build my church; and the gates of hell shall not prevail against it" (Matthew 16:15). The Prophet Joseph taught that the "rock" is the rock of revelation (*Teachings*, 274).

Fourth, revelation is the only way for man to know God. Paul, in writing to the Corinthians, said, "For what man knoweth the things of a man, save the spirit of man which is in him? even so the things of God knoweth no man, but the Spirit of God" (1 Corinthians 2:11).

Finally, there are counterfeit revelations that can come from Satan or from our own emotions. I have heard youth and adults sometimes equate the spirituality of a meeting with the number of tears it caused; the more tears shed, the more spiritual the meeting. This concerns me. The fact that tears often accompany the workings of the spirit certainly doesn't mean that an experience which doesn't cause tears is not a spiritual experience. Elder Boyd K. Packer, an Apostle, said, "Be ever on guard lest you be deceived by inspiration from an unworthy source. You can be given false spiritual messages. There are counterfeit spirits just as there are counterfeit angels. . . . The spiritual part of us and the emotional part of us are so closely linked that it is possible to mistake an emotional impulse for something spiritual. We occasionally find people who receive what they assume to be spiritual promptings from God, when those promptings are either centered in the emotions or are from the adversary" ("The Candle of the Lord," *Ensign*, Jan. 1983, 55–56).

Now that we have a little understanding of what revelation is, let's examine those principles that govern the giving and receiving of revelation. First: the Lord, not us, determines who receives revelation, when it is given, how it is given, and what is revealed. It's almost as though some people tell the Lord, "If this church is true, have my sister from California call me tonight." We cannot decide what answer we require or in what form it will come. The Savior gave us a great pattern when he said, "If it be possible, let this cup pass from me: nevertheless, not as I will, but as thou wilt" (Matthew 26:39).

Students often wonder why they do not see the Lord like Saul did, or why they are not visited by an angel, like Alma the Younger was, or even why they are not struck dumb like King Lamoni was. It's true that some people are converted in a remarkable manner, yet most testimonies aren't gained in such a way (see 3 Nephi 9:20).

Most revelation comes through the quiet whisperings of the Spirit; the sensational and dramatic spiritual experiences are real, but they are the exception rather than the rule.

Speaking of the still small voice, Elder Boyd K. Packer said, "Occasionally it will press just firmly enough for us to pay heed. But most of the time, if we do not heed the gentle feeling, the Spirit will withdraw and wait until we come seeking and listening" ("The Candle of the Lord," p. 53). President Spencer W. Kimball said, "Even in our day, many people . . . expect if there be revelation it will come with an awe-inspiring, earth-shaking display . . . The burning bushes, the smoking mountains, the sheets [full of] of four-footed beasts, the Cumorahs, and the Kirtlands were realities; but they were the exceptions. The great volume of revelation came to Moses and to Joseph and comes to today's prophet in the less spectacular way— that of deep impressions, without spectacle or glamour or dramatic events. Always expecting the spectacular, many will miss entirely the constant flow of revealed communication" (in Munich Germany Area Conference, 1973, 76–77).

And today, President Ezra Taft Benson has counseled that for every Lamoni, or Paul, "there are hundreds and thousands of people who find the process of repentance much more subtle, much more imperceptible. Day by day, they move closer to the Lord, little realizing they are building a godlike life" ("A Mighty Change of Heart," *Ensign*, Oct. 1989, 5).

Another factor that influences the reception of revelation is worthiness. Revelation is more readily given as we meet the personal conditions the Lord stipulates. We must submit our will to God, strive to be diligent, study the scriptures and the words of the modern prophets, and strive to be meek and lowly of heart. We need to learn from the experiences of Laman and Lemuel that due to wickedness, we can actually become "past feeling" and lose the capacity to hear the still, small voice prompting us (see 1 Nephi 17:45).

On one occasion, Oliver Cowdery desired to translate rather than act as scribe to the Prophet Joseph. He was not successful in his attempt, and was told by the Lord, "You took no thought save it was to ask me" (D&C 9:7). Not only do some "just ask," but they ask when the answers are already found in the scriptures and the words of the prophets. Elder Harold B. Lee, an Apostle, said, "It should not be necessary today for us to expect new written revelation on every point when we have these men [the Apostles and prophets] thus possessed of the same spirit of revelation. A brief review of the past instruction of our leaders should only serve to warn the disobedient and to encourage the obedient to continue faithful" (in Conference Report, Oct. 1941, 114).

Remember the Lord reveals His will to us in His own due time. We should not put time constraints or demands on the Lord. I feel it would be unwise to tell the Lord "I need an answer by Thursday or I will assume the answer is no." Elder Boyd K. Packer said, "It is not wise to wrestle with the revelations with such insistence as to demand immediate answers or blessings to your liking. You cannot force spiritual things. Such words as compel, coerce, constrain, pressure, demand, do not describe our privileges with the Spirit. You can no more force the Spirit to respond than you can force a bean to sprout, or an egg to hatch before its time. You can create a climate to foster growth, nourish, and protect; but you cannot force or compel: you must await the growth. Do not be impatient to gain great spiritual knowledge. Let it grow, help it grow, but do not force it or you will open the way to be misled" ("The Candle of the Lord," 53).

The Lord has blessed each of us with many talents and expects us to use those talents to do many things of our own free will (D&C 58:26–29). Elder Dallin H. Oaks, an Apostle, said, "The Spirit of the Lord is not likely to give us revelations on matters that are trivial. I once heard a young woman in a testimony meeting praise the spirituality of her husband, indicating that he submitted every question to the Lord. She told how he accompanied her shopping and would not even choose between different brands of canned vegetables without making his selection a matter of prayer. That strikes me as improper. I believe the Lord expects us to use our intelligence and experience he has given us to make these kinds of choices" (*Speeches of the Year!* [Provo: Brigham Young University Press, 1982], 26). Even the Lord has said on occasion that it "mattereth not" to Him on some items people are concerned with (D&C 60:5).

A frequently asked question is, "How can I discern between true revelation and its counterfeits?" In today's world there are many people claiming to be speaking for God. There are a few principles that need to be understood if we are to avoid deception.

First, the Spirit does not cause us to act in ways that are bizarre or out of harmony with the sacred nature of God. The scriptures teach "He that preacheth and he that receiveth, understand one another, and both are edified and rejoice together. And that which doth not edify is not of God, and is darkness" (D&C 50:22–23). The Prophet Joseph taught that false spirits are found in The Church of Jesus Christ of Latter-day Saints. He mentioned on one occasion that:

> Soon after the Gospel was established in Kirtland, and during the absence of the authorities of the Church, many false spirits were introduced, many strange visions were seen, and wild, enthusiastic notions were entertained; men ran out of doors under the influence of this spirit, and some of them got upon the stumps of trees and shouted, and all kinds of extravagances were entered into by them; one man pursued a ball that he said he saw flying in the air, until he came to a precipice, when he jumped into the top of a tree, which saved his life; and many ridiculous things were entered into, calculated to bring disgrace upon the Church of God, to cause the Spirit of God to be withdrawn, and to uproot and destroy those glorious principles which had been developed for the salvation of the

human family (*Discourses of the Prophet Joseph Smith,* comp. Alma P. Burton [Salt Lake City: Deseret Book Co., 1965], 92).

The Prophet Joseph further taught that what we sometimes assume are ministering angels in the Church are in reality Satan and those cast out with him, who can appear as angels of light. He told the story of a sister in New York who had a vision and was told that if she would walk to a certain place in the woods an angel would appear to her. The Prophet continued:

> She went at the appointed time, and saw a glorious person-age descending, arrayed in white, with sandy colored hair; he commenced and told her to fear God, and said that her husband was called to do great things, but that he must not go more than one hundred miles from home, or he would not return; whereas God had called him to go to the ends of the earth, and he has since been more than one thousand miles from home, and is yet alive. Many true things were spoken by this personage, and many things that were false. How, it may be asked, was this known to be a bad angel? By the color of his hair; that is one of the signs that he can be known by, and by his contradicting a former revelation (*Discourses,* 93).

We need to understand then that a true messenger from our Father in Heaven would not contradict truths already revealed.

Next, we need to understand that revelation comes through certain channels. Our Heavenly Father's house is a house of order. Elder Dallin H. Oaks, said, "Only the president of the Church receives revelation to guide the entire Church. Only the stake president receives revelation for the special guidance of the stake. The person who receives revelation for the ward is the bishop. For a family, it is the priesthood leadership of the family. Individuals can receive revelation to guide their own lives. But when one person purports to receive revelation for another person outside his or her own stewardship—such as a Church member who claims to have revelation to guide the entire Church or a person who claims to have revelation to guide another person over whom he or she has no presiding authority according to the order of the Church—you can be sure that such revelations are not from the Lord" ("Revelation," 1982, 25). When we follow our priesthood leaders, they will help us recognize revelation from our Father in Heaven.

Elder Bruce R. McConkie, said, "Would you like a formula to tell you how to get personal revelation? It might be written in many ways. My formula is simply this: 1. Search the scriptures 2. Keep the commandments 3. Ask in faith.

"Any person who will do this will get his heart so in tune with the Infinite that there will come into his being, from the 'still small voice' the eternal realities of religion. And as he progresses and advances and comes nearer to God, there will be a day when he will entertain angels, when he will see visions, and the final end is to view the face of God" (Bruce R. McConkie, *How to Get Personal Revelation,* Brigham Young University Speeches of the Year [Provo, 11 Oct. 1966], 6).

I believe the following poem by Edwin Markham best summarizes the step by step, line by line process of receiving revelation. The poem reads:

The builder who first bridged Niagara's gorge
Before he swung his cable shore to shore
Sent out across the gulf his venturing kite
Bearing a slender cord from unseen hands
To grasp upon the further cliff and draw
A greater cord, and then a greater yet,
Till at last across the chasm swung
The cable—then mighty bridge in air.

So we may send our little timid thoughts
Across the void, out to God's reaching hands—
Send out our love and faith to thread the deep—
Thought after thought until the little cord

Has greatened to a chain no chance can break.
And we are anchored to the infinite.

We need to next address how we should treat those special, spiritual experiences we have in our lives. The scriptures give us great counsel when they say "Remember that that which cometh from above is sacred, and must be spoken with care, and by constraint of the Spirit; and in this there is no condemnation, and ye receive the Spirit through prayer; wherefore, without this there remaineth condemnation" (D&C 63:64). Elder Boyd K. Packer said, "I have come to believe also that it is not wise to continually talk of unusual spiritual experiences. They are to be guarded with care and shared only when the Spirit itself prompts you to use them to the blessing of others" ("The Candle of the Lord," 53).

Lastly, now that we understand some of the principles upon which the receipt of revelation is based, what is our responsibility upon receiving promptings from the Spirit? Alma teaches us that if we don't accept God's word when it is given, we may lose what we have (see Alma 12:9–12). Brigham Young stated, "When a revelation is given to any people, they must walk according to it, or suffer the penalty which is the punishment of disobedience" (*Journal of Discourses,* 12:127). Elder Boyd K. Packer told a personal experience wherein he suffered the consequences of not following the promptings of the Spirit. He said:

> I had been prompted several times, for the good of the work, to release one of my counselors. Besides praying about it, I had reasoned that it was the right thing to do. But I did not do it. I feared that it would injure a man who had given long service to the Church.
>
> The Spirit withdrew from me. I could get no promptings on who should be called as a counselor should I release him. It lasted for several weeks. My prayers seemed to be contained within the room where I offered them. I tried a number of alternate ways to arrange the work, but to no avail. Finally, I did as

I was bidden to do by the Spirit. Immediately, the gift returned! Oh, the exquisite sweetness to have the gift again. You know it, for you have it, the gift of the Holy Ghost. And the brother was not injured, indeed he was greatly blessed and immediately thereafter the work prospered ("The Candle of the Lord," 55).

I hope that as each of us strives to gain a stronger testimony of Jesus Christ and his gospel, we will reflect upon these principles. The only way a person can know that the gospel of Jesus Christ and this Church are true is by personal revelation. I pray that we will ponder the scriptures and the words of the prophets and Apostles. Then, as we are privileged to receive the promptings of that "still, small voice"—the Holy Ghost, we will follow them.

Randall C. Bird is manager of seminary curriculum for the Church Educational System. He is a sports enthusiast, and during his high school years was named to the Idaho all-state teams in football and track. He has been a high school coach in both sports. He also enjoys fishing, collecting sports memorabilia, reading, and being with his family. He has served as a stake president. He and his wife, Carla, are the parents of six children.

11

"I THINK I CAN" AND OTHER BRAVE THOUGHTS

Vickey Pahnke

There was this little train. Actually, he was an engine. As he approached a steep incline, he thought, *There is no way I can make it up this mountain.* Then he had another thought: *Maybe I need to change my attitude. Instead of thinking I can't do this, perhaps I should think about how I can do it.* So the little engine repeated to himself, "I think I can; I think I can; I think I can." Slowly he crept up the mountain. With his focus on making it to the top, he paid less attention to the difficulty of making the ascent. With a lot of effort and a lot of "I think I can" thoughts, the brave little engine made it to the top. That is how he came to be known as "the little engine that could."

My parents told or read that story to me lots of times when I was small. But it wasn't until I got bigger and older that I had a more clear understanding of the significance of that little engine. He had stamina. He had a good attitude. He had conviction. He had courage. Now, as I navigate life's mountains and valleys, I try to keep a picture of that little stalwart engine clearly in my mind, because life can be difficult and full of challenges. But doesn't it feel great when we hang in there, hold on, and make it through the heartbreak of the hour or up that mountain of the moment?

I want to share with you a few brave thoughts about hanging in there and holding on, about finding the courage and strength to do what is right, about conquering the mountains that loom ahead and rejoicing at overcoming the obstacles that lie in our path. These are things that I need to continually work on as I chug along the track that leads home. I am hoping they might be of help to you, too.

The Courage to Make a Difference

If life ever feels a little overwhelming, like it does for me on occasion, these are the times to decide that you won't let problems keep you down. We have to be careful not to wallow in a pity party: you know, that special party at which you are the only guest and everything is terrible and depressing and awful. If the way we react to life's challenges can make or break us, I hope we will react like my friend Jason. Jason was an athletic young man with a promising future in baseball. On a trip to Lake Powell, he dove into the water, hit his head on a boulder, and became a quadriplegic. The entire story of his fight to survive and live a useful life is beautiful and inspiring. But it is especially interesting that Jason's practical, day-to-day method of making a difference in his own life is to get rid of the pity party. He says that he limits the whining time to thirty minutes. When the half hour is up, so is the complaining. It has made a big difference for the better in his life. Because of his courage and determination, he has made a difference in a lot of other lives also! The following poem perfectly sums up Jason's philosophy:

The Oyster
There once was an oyster
Whose story I tell,
Who found that some sand
Had got into his shell.
It was only a grain,
But it gave him great pain
For oysters have feelings
Although they're so plain.

Now, did he berate
The harsh workings of fate
That had brought him
To such a deplorable state?
Did he curse at the government,
Cry for election,
And claim that the sea should
Have given him protection?

No—he said to himself
As he lay on a shell,
Since I cannot remove it
I shall try to improve it.
Now the years have rolled around,
As the years always do,
And he came to his ultimate
Destiny: stew.

And the small grain of sand
That had bothered him so
Was a beautiful pearl
All richly aglow.
Now the tale has a moral,
For isn't it grand
What an oyster can do
With a morsel of sand?

What couldn't we do
If we'd only begin
With some of the things
That get under our skin.

(Anonymous)

Elder Boyd K. Packer of the Quorum of the Twelve Apostles said, "Things we cannot solve, we must survive" ("Balm of Gilead,"

Ensign, November 1987, 18). When the going gets tough—and it will from time to time—we can pick ourselves up and decide not only to get through it but to get through it well. The very act of getting honorably through the difficulties strengthens our testimony, builds our courage, and keeps us pushing up the mountain.

The Courage to Say No

Joseph is a priesthood leader I am eager to one day meet. Here is a guy who happens to have a lot going for him. He has the good fortune of being highly favored by his father. His dad even gives him a beautiful coat of many colors. This doesn't go over too well with his brothers. For being favored, he has the bad fortune of being dumped in a hole and sold as a slave by his brothers. He has the good fortune of being rescued—well, kind of; read Genesis 37 to get the rest of the story—and ends up in the king's court. He has the bad fortune of being good-looking (stay with me; yes, it seems it can be a problem sometimes). Potiphar's wife thinks to herself, *This is one good-looking guy* (or something like that) and sets out to seduce him. He has the good sense to say no (see Genesis 39).

Let's stop here for a moment. Joseph was a human being. He surely had feelings and desires and thoughts like other human beings. Potiphar's wife was a powerful woman. Who would know if he gave in to her advances? But Joseph had the courage to say no. He was falsely accused and had the bad fortune of being sent to prison. As we continue reading Genesis 40 we find he has the good fortune of being blessed with the ability to interpret dreams. And because of this ability, he comes full circle: back to the king's court and able to save himself and even his brothers who, so many years before, deserted him. One of the powerful elements in this story is the continual good fortune and bad fortune Joseph encounters throughout his life. He used them all to his good because he had courage. What an example Joseph is!

Let's look at a modern-day example of the courage to say no.

Scott was the only member of the LDS Church in his high school. He took a lot of teasing and dealt daily with classmates who dared him to join their weekly drinking parties. There was a big event coming up on Friday night. Everyone wanted Scott to climb down off his pedestal and "be a man," or in other words become a beer drinker. What would it matter if he bent the rules just once? Who would care if he broke the Word of Wisdom just this one time?

Friday was a tense day for Scott as he tried to rationalize his decision to attend the party. He lied to his parents about where he was going and headed off to try new things. The party was pretty crazy. Scott was afraid to do something that he knew was wrong, but he was more afraid of looking bad in front of his friends. Someone passed him a drink. All eyes were on him. With his heart pounding, he raised the cup to his mouth. And then he remembered something he had heard President Howard W. Hunter say: "Courage is acting in spite of fear" (Conference Report, April 1967, 117). Scott slowly set down the cup and walked out of the party. He had found the courage to say no.

I wish I could tell you that Scott's high school days were great and everyone applauded him for his decision to act on what he knew was right. The truth is, he was the laughingstock of the junior class. Very few ventured to become his friend. But Scott remained true and faithful. He served a mission and married in the temple. But that isn't the neatest part of the story.

Scott has a younger brother. Jared never had the strength of conviction that seemed to come naturally to Scott. He thought his big brother was a nerd and a loser. But he quietly watched his older brother. More times than Scott would ever know, his good example paved the way for a little brother who remembered the courage of his older sibling. Jared was present at a youth conference where I was teaching. He credited his brother's strength in saying no to improper things for keeping him from going way off track. Tears came to my eyes as I listened to a teenage boy express his love and admiration for the courage of his older brother.

"Sister Pahnke," Jared said, "my brother taught me a scripture that goes, 'Be strong and of a good courage' [Deuteronomy 31:6]. But he didn't just teach me with words; he taught me by his own example."

I thought of another older brother—our Savior—and the perfect example of courage he has provided for us. Have the courage to say no to the things of this world, my friends. The mountains will be easier to climb if you do!

The Courage to Say Yes

We read these powerful words in Deuteronomy 20:1: "When thou goest out to battle against thine enemies, . . . be not afraid of them: for the Lord thy God is with thee."

Moses was a man who knew more than a little about courage, wouldn't you say? Think quickly over his life: being placed in a basket and sent down a river as an infant to escape certain death; being raised by Pharoah's daughter as royalty yet forsaking it for his higher calling; being outcast; dealing with huge numbers of Israelites who weren't willing to follow the Lord's commandments, even after they had been led out of Egypt; facing Pharoah full of faith to show the Lord's power. Moses was a man who understood going into battle against enemies. Again and again he could have said no when it must have seemed hard to say yes: Yes, I will have faith enough to get the chosen people across the Red Sea; Yes, I will lead this group of people out of bondage even though many of them are ungrateful and disobedient; Yes, I will do the things the Lord commands me. I want to meet Moses one day. I want to ask him questions and shake his hand and maybe give him a hug, if he'll let me! He provides wonderful examples of the courage to say yes.

Whether you need that courage to say yes to a calling, yes to helping out when a family member or friend needs you and it's inconvenient or bothersome, or yes in any situation when it might be easier to say no, you are building steam in that testimony engine of yours to get through the obstacles in this life.

The Courage to Wait

As a young teenager, I wrote down a quote I found in an old book: "To wait on God, no time is lost—wait on." There have been a number of times when I have prayed fervently for something and the answer was slow in coming. As I think back it becomes clear to me that I needed the wait. Finding and utilizing patience was necessary for the development of my character. And the Lord's time is different—and infinitely better—than our own. The waiting, or enduring, gives us an extra push as we trek up our mountains.

President Ezra Taft Benson counseled us, "Daily, constantly, we choose by our desires, our thoughts, and our actions whether we want to be blessed or cursed, happy or miserable. One of the trials of life is that we do not usually receive immediately the full blessing for righteousness or the full cursing for wickedness. That it will come is certain, but ofttimes there is a waiting period that occurs. . . . During this testing time the righteous must continue to love God, trust in His promises, be patient, and be assured" ("The Great Commandment—Love the Lord," *Ensign,* May 1988, 6).

My young brothers and sisters, we chose to follow the Savior in our premortal state. We honorably and courageously fought for the privilege of coming into this mortal state. If things are difficult for you right now, hold steady and stay on track. If you are experiencing no problems and it is smooth sailing for you, enjoy it. It will most certainly change. The bumps and potholes and obstacles are the very things that help us develop the stamina and attitude and courage to continue on this earthly journey. As we seek first the kingdom of God (see Matthew 6:33), we may be amazed at how we are able to hang in there and hold on.

God bless us to think brave thoughts, adjust our attitudes, and make the required effort to succeed. May he assist us as we muster up the courage to say yes when needed and no when appropriate, to make a difference in our own lives as well as in the lives of those around us, and to wait for the perfect direction of the Father as he directs us along our onward track.

Vickey Pahnke studied musical theater at Brigham Young University after joining the Church as a teenager. She later received a master's degree in communications. She works as a songwriter, producer, and author. Vickey and her husband, Bob, are the parents of four children. She has been involved with many of the BYU youth programs—such as Especially for Youth, Best of Especially for Youth, and Outreach youth conferences— and has been a speaker for the Know Your Religion and BYU Education Week series. She loves mountains, laughter, the ocean, kids of all ages, music, food, and cooking. But mostly, she loves being a mom.

12

ACT III: LIFE AFTER DEATH

Todd Parker

Each year thousands of people visit Temple Square and tour the visitors' center there. Many visitors watch the Church-produced movie, *Man's Search for Happiness,* narrated by Elder Richard L. Evans. The movie depicts a family with young children and a grandfather who lives with them. Eventually, the grandfather dies. As the family stands by the snowy grave of their beloved grandfather, Richard L. Evans's comforting voice says: "Like every member of the human race, you were born and you must die. Your birth is a matter of record; you take it for granted. But death, that uncertain door that leads ahead, has been for man an awesome mystery. Life's greatest test comes with the death of a loved one; and without faith in the immortality of the soul, the separation of death looms forever comfortless."

To help us understand what to expect after this life, President Boyd K. Packer addressed the youth of the Church and compared life to a three-act play. Act I is the premortal existence; Act II, mortality; and Act III, life after death (see "The Play and the Plan," May 7, 1995, CES Satellite Broadcast). He explained that by understanding this plan we can gain a better perspective of our purpose in life and what to expect in the life to come. To help broaden our perspective for Act III, we will consider questions often asked by both youth and adult members of the Church. The answers to these questions will be based on passages of scripture and statements that have been made by the General Authorities.

In the postmortal world, there are two major divisions: the spirit world and the Resurrection. We'll begin first with questions about the spirit world.

What Happens at Death?

From the Doctrine and Covenants we learn that "the spirit and the body are the soul of man" (88:15). James, the Lord's brother, wrote in the New Testament, "The body without the spirit is dead" (James 2:26). At death, the body and the spirit separate. The body returns to the earth, but the spirit enters a new realm called the spirit world. In the movie, *Man's Search for Happiness,* Elder Evans described it this way: "After death, though your mortal body lies in the earth, you, your spirit self, being eternal, continues to live. Your memory of this life will remain with you and the knowledge of your life before birth will be restored. Like coming out of a darkened room into the light, through death you will emerge into a place of reawakening and find loved ones, waiting to welcome you."

Where Is the Spirit World?

Brigham Young asked this question himself and answered it this way:

"Where is the Spirit World?—Is the spirit world here? It is not beyond the sun, but is on this earth that was organized for the people that have lived and that do and will live upon it. . . .

"When you lay down this tabernacle, where are you going? Into the spiritual world. Are you going into Abraham's bosom [meaning the presence of God]? No, not anywhere nigh there but into the spirit world. Where is the spirit world? It is right here. Do the good and evil spirits go together? Yes, they do. Do they both inhabit one kingdom? Yes, they do. Do they go to the sun? No. Do they go beyond the boundaries of the organized earth? No, they do not. . . .

"If the Lord would permit it, and it was his will that it should be done, you could see the spirits that have departed from this world, as plainly as you now see bodies with your natural eyes" (*Discourses of Brigham Young,* sel. John A. Widtsoe [1946], 376–77).

Elder Parley P. Pratt wrote of the spirit world: "It is here on the very planet where we were born, or in other words, the earth and other planets of a like sphere have their inward or spiritual spheres as well as their outward, or temporal. The one is peopled by temporal tabernacles, and the other by spirits. A veil is drawn between the one sphere and the other whereby all the objects in the spiritual sphere are rendered invisible to those in the temporal" (*Key to the Science of Theology* [1978], 81).

Some people mistakenly believe that at death we enter the presence of God. This is not the case. As resurrected beings, God and Christ dwell in a celestial world apart from this one. Heber C. Kimball said: "As for my going into the immediate presence of God when I die, I do not expect it, but I expect to go into the world of spirits and associate with my brethren, and preach the Gospel in the spiritual world, and prepare myself in every necessary way to receive my body again, and then enter through the wall into the celestial world. I never shall come into the presence of my Father and God until I have received my resurrected body, neither will any other person" (*Journal of Discourses,* 3:112–13).

The postmortal spirit world is a place of residence for those who have died and are awaiting resurrection when their spirits and bodies will unite again. Life in the spirit world is an intermediate condition between earth life and life as a resurrected being.

What Is It Like in the Spirit World?

The Lord revealed to Joseph Smith: "There is no such thing as immaterial matter. All spirit is matter, but it is more fine or pure, and can only be discerned by purer eyes; we cannot see it; but when our bodies are purified we shall see that it is all matter" (D&C 131:7–8).

The spirit world is very similar to this world but in another dimension. Although it's here on this earth and we cannot see it with our natural eyes, it exists. It has the kinds of things we have in the world. In that world there are spirit bushes, trees, lakes, buildings, flowers, etc. Brigham Young said, "Spirits are just as familiar with spirits as bodies are with bodies, though spirits are composed of matter so refined as not to be tangible to this coarser organization" (*Discourses of Brigham Young*, 379).

Once when he was very ill, Jedediah Grant's spirit left his body. President Heber C. Kimball later went to visit him and recalled what Brother Grant told him in these words: "He said to me, 'Brother Heber, I have been into the spirit world two nights in succession, and, of all the dreads that ever came across me, the worst was to have to again return to my body, though I had to do it.' But 'O,' says he, 'the order and government that were there! When in the spirit world, I saw the order of righteous men and women. . . . ' He said that the people he there saw were organized in family capacities; and . . . all were organized and in perfect harmony. . . .

"He saw the righteous gathered together in the spirit world, and there were no wicked spirits among them. He saw his wife; she was the first person that came to him. He saw many that he knew, but did not have conversation with any except his wife Caroline. She came to him, and he said that she looked beautiful and had their little child, that died on the Plains, in her arms, and said, 'Mr. Grant, here is little Margaret; you know that the wolves ate her up, but it did not hurt her; here she is all right.' . . .

"He also spoke of the buildings he saw there, remarking that the Lord gave Solomon wisdom and poured gold and silver into his hands that he might display his skill and ability, and said that the temple erected by Solomon was much inferior to the most ordinary buildings he saw in the spirit world.

"'In regard to gardens,' says Brother Grant, 'I have seen good gardens on this earth, but I never saw any to compare with those that were there. I saw flowers of numerous kinds, and some with fifty to a hundred different colored flowers growing upon one stalk'" (*Journal of Discourses,* 4:135–36).

Is It Different in the Spirit World for the Righteous and the Wicked?

In the Book of Mormon, the prophet Alma wrote: "Now, concerning the state of the soul between death and the resurrection . . . the spirits of those who are righteous are received into a state of happiness, which is called paradise, a state of rest, a state of peace, where they shall rest from all their troubles and from all care, and sorrow.

"And then shall it come to pass, that the spirits of the wicked, yea, who are evil—for behold, they have no part nor portion of the Spirit of the Lord; for behold, they chose evil works rather than good; . . . there shall be weeping, and wailing, and gnashing of teeth, and this because of their own iniquity, being led captive by the will of the devil.

"Now this is the state of the souls of the wicked, yea, in darkness, and a state of awful, fearful looking for the fiery indignation of the wrath of God upon them; thus they remain in this state, as well as the righteous in paradise, until the time of their resurrection" (Alma 40:11–14).

When the righteous die, they enter a state or condition referred to as paradise. It is a state of rest and waiting where they are free from the pains and sorrows of this world. But not all people will immediately experience this state of rest in paradise. The wicked enter a condition called spirit prison or "hell" where they suffer spiritual torment as a consequence of the sins they have not repented of while on earth. It seems more accurate to consider these two states as *conditions* rather than *places.* The prophets have taught that the wicked and the righteous (since the time of Christ's visit to the spirit world while his body was in the tomb) go to the same place at death.

President Brigham Young explained it this way: "The Prophet lays down his body, he lays down his life, and his spirit goes to the world of spirits; the persecutor of the Prophet dies, and he goes to Hades; they both go to one place, and they are not to be separated yet. Now understand, that this is part of the great sermon the Lord is preaching in his providence, the righteous and the wicked are together in Hades" (*Discourses of Brigham Young,* 377).

Remember, the spirit world is like this world. It is actually an extension of this world. Just as the righteous and the unrighteous live in the same cities, walk on the same streets, shop in the same stores, and are not physically separated in this world, the same is true in the spirit world. Just as the righteous tend to meet and congregate together in this sphere, the righteous spirits in the spirit world tend to congregate there also. And just as one person could be living in a state of happiness (paradise) in his house here in mortality, another person in the same city could be living in a condition of "hell" as a result of the consequences of immorality, drug abuse, or alcoholism.

What Do People Do in the Spirit World?

In an article entitled "The Spirit World, Our Next Home," printed in the January 1977 *Ensign,* Dale Mouritsen explained: "Apparently, righteous people in the spirit world are organized just as they are here, arranged in families and quorums. Priesthood operates there as it operates here." President Brigham Young declared: "When the faithful Elders, holding this Priesthood, go into the spirit world they carry with them the same power and Priesthood that they had while in the mortal tabernacle" (*Discourses of Brigham Young,* 132; see also D&C 124:130). The blessings of the priesthood are thus present in the spirit world. One elder who passed beyond the veil and returned spoke of the order he saw there:

"While I was in the spirit world, I observed that the people there were busy, and that they were perfectly organized for the work they were doing. It seemed to me a continuation of the work we are doing here—something like going from one stake to another. There was nothing there that seemed particularly strange to me, everything being natural" (Peter E. Johnson, *Relief Society Magazine,* August 1920, 455).

Is the Spirit World Exactly like This One or Are There Some Differences There?

Apparently, some things are quite different. In this world we are very conditioned to view things in a past, present, or future setting. Time is different there. Brigham Young described it in these words: "The brightness and glory of the next apartment is inexpressible. It is not encumbered so that when we advance in years we have to be stubbing along and be careful lest we fall down. . . . But yonder, how different! They move with ease and like lightning. . . . If we want to behold Jerusalem as it was in the days of the Savior; or if we want to see the Garden of Eden as it was when created, there we are, and we see it as it existed spiritually, for it was created first spiritually and then temporally, and spiritually it still remains. And when there we may behold the earth as at the dawn of creation, or we may visit any city we please that exists upon its surface" (*Discourses of Brigham Young,* 380).

How Long Does a Person Stay in the Spirit World?

The answer to this question depends on certain things, such as when you lived, how righteous you were, and if you have sins of which you have not repented. The spirit world basically is a place of waiting for resurrection. Since different people are resurrected at different times, the amount of time one waits in the spirit world varies. There is a definite order to the resurrection (see D&C 88:97–102). A person is resurrected when his or her spirit is reunited with his body. Generally speaking, the resurrection from death begins with the very best, Jesus Christ, and ends with the very worst, the sons of perdition. There are two parts of the resurrection: the first resurrection—also called the resurrection of life—and the last resurrection—

also called the "resurrection of damnation" (John 5:29). The first resurrection serves two categories of people: the "morning" of the first resurrection (for those raised to a celestial inheritance) and the "afternoon" of the first resurrection (which will provide a terrestrial inheritance for those so qualified). The last resurrection will serve two categories of people: those who have lived telestial lives and those who have become sons of perdition.

The order of the resurrection involves not only the four categories of people just mentioned but designates also different times when they come forth from their graves.

The Apostle Paul reminds us that Christ was the first to be resurrected (see 1 Corinthians 15:20), and the Doctrine and Covenants further teaches that certain righteous people who lived from the time of Adam down to the time of Christ were "with Christ in his resurrection" (133:55; see also Alma 40:18–19). The resurrection of these people took place during what is called the morning of the first resurrection. This resurrection will continue when Christ comes in his glory at the time of his second coming. Those resurrected at that time will be said to have also come forth in the morning of the first resurrection.

During this same time the telestial people of the earth will be burned by the brightness of the coming of Christ (see D&C 5:19). Following the burning of the wicked and the resurrection of the celestial people, the terrestrial people who have died will then be resurrected. This will happen during what is called the afternoon of the first resurrection. Having died, the telestial people and sons of perdition will remain in the spirit world during the 1,000 years of the Millennium. At the end of the Millennium, these souls will finally come forth from the graves as part of the last resurrection.

What Will Our Bodies Be like When We Are Resurrected?

We will be resurrected with tangible bodies of flesh and bone (not blood), quickened by the spirit, just as Jesus was (see Luke

24:36–39). Our resurrected body will resemble our mortal body but will be an immortal, perfected body (see Alma 11:45; 40:23). Some people mistakenly believe that we will be resurrected with only spirit bodies. This belief results from an incorrect interpretation of Paul's letter to the Corinthians where he states, "Flesh and blood cannot inherit the kingdom of God" (1 Corinthians 15:50).

Joseph Smith helped clarify Paul's writing when he stated, "God Almighty Himself dwells in eternal fire; flesh and blood cannot go there, for all corruption is devoured by the fire. . . . When our flesh is quickened by the Spirit, there will be no blood in this tabernacle" (*Teachings of the Prophet Joseph Smith,* 367). On another occasion Joseph taught, "Flesh and blood cannot go there; but flesh and bones, quickened by the Spirit of God, can" (*Teachings of the Prophet Joseph Smith,* 326).

Once we are raised from the dead, our bodies will be either celestial, terrestrial, or telestial in nature (see 1 Corinthians 15:40–42; D&C 88:27–31), depending on the type of life we have chosen to live.

So when we appear at the "final judgment" there will be no surprise as to which kingdom we will inherit since we will already be resurrected with one of the three types of bodies. In essence we will "wear our judgment to court."

Resurrection is a priesthood ordinance. Just as a person must be baptized and then be ordained with authority in order to baptize others, so also must a person be resurrected and then ordained by one holding the proper priesthood keys to be able to perform this ordinance (see Spencer W. Kimball, *Ensign,* May 1977, 49). What a blessing it will be to worthy priesthood holders to perform this ordinance for deceased loved ones of their families.

To summarize then, the third act of this eternal play has two parts: the spirit world and the resurrection. How we live in Act II and the choices we make here will determine where we'll be and what we'll be doing in Act III. For the wicked, there awaits sorrow, punishment, and remorse in the spirit world and a resurrection to a telestial order. For the righteous, the spirit world will be a place of rest and peace, awaiting a glorious resurrection. Ours is the freedom to choose.

Todd Parker received his bachelor's degree in English from Weber State College. His received an M.Ed. degree in counseling and an Ed.D. degree in educational psychology, both from Brigham Young University. He is currently an associate professor at BYU in the Department of Ancient Scripture and has served as a bishop. He has written curriculum materials for the Church Educational System and has taught seminary and institute. He and his wife, Debra, are the parents of six boys and three girls. Todd enjoys running and pole vaulting and had a distinguished track and field career.

13

FEASTING UPON THE WORD

R. Scott Simmons

A nd that from a child thou hast known the holy scriptures, which are able to make thee wise unto salvation through faith which is in Christ Jesus.

"All scripture is given by inspiration of God, and is profitable for doctrine, for reproof, for correction, for instruction in righteousness" (2 Timothy 3:15–16).

I love the scriptures. I have reached a point in my life where it is difficult for me to let a day go by without reading my scriptures. For me, if I miss a day of reading, it's like going without food—spiritually speaking. The hunger that I experience is real and needs to be satisfied. I have found that the only way to completely satisfy this hunger is to "feast upon the words of Christ" (2 Nephi 32:3).

I feel this way now, but it wasn't always the case. There was a time when I really struggled to read the scriptures. As a result, I was starving spiritually, and I didn't realize it.

My struggle came when I was about your age. I had been taught that the scriptures were important, and so I tried to read them. However, I found the language hard to understand—all the thees, thous, and thines, not to mention all the different names and places I couldn't pronounce. Also, there were many places where I just didn't get what was going on. I was often frustrated and would just stop reading. Then, I would hear a lesson or a talk on the importance of the scriptures and try reading again, only to end up frustrated once more.

All the while, I was really struggling personally. I didn't realize it at the time, but my struggles were a result of spiritual malnutrition. I was hungry for something but didn't know what it was. Does any of this sound familiar, even a little? If it does, maybe I can help. As I said, things are completely different now. The language is still tough to decipher sometimes, and there are even times when I am still not sure what is going on, but I don't get frustrated. I even enjoy those difficult scriptures, even though I admit I don't completely understand them. So what made the difference? Let me show you.

First, I know you already know the scriptures are important, but do you know just how important? Here is what President Ezra Taft Benson had to say: "Success in righteousness, the power to avoid deception and resist temptation, guidance in our daily lives, healing of the soul—these are but a few of the promises the Lord has given to those who will come to His word. Does the Lord promise and not fulfill? Surely if He tells us that these things will come to us if we lay hold upon His word, then the blessings can be ours. And if we do not, then the blessings may be lost. *However diligent we may be in other areas, certain blessings are to be found only in the scriptures, only in coming to the word of the Lord and holding fast to it as we make our way through the mists of darkness to the tree of life*" (*Ensign,* May 1986, 82; emphasis added).

Did you catch what President Benson said at the end of this quote? "Certain blessings are to be found only in the scriptures." That is important to note. You can be doing everything else right, but if you are not reading your scriptures, you are missing out on some important blessings. Just what are those blessings? President Benson gives a clue at the end of his quote. Did you notice he mentioned the tree of life? What does that have to do with scripture reading?

Remember Father Lehi's vision? In it he saw "a tree, whose

fruit was desirable to make one happy. . . . And as [he] partook of
the fruit thereof it filled [his] soul with exceedingly great joy"
(1 Nephi 8:10, 12).

A tree bearing fruit that will make you happy and fill your soul
with joy? Sounds good, doesn't it? Later on, Nephi tells us what this
tree and fruit represent. He says, "It is the love of God, which shed-
deth itself abroad in the hearts of the children of men; wherefore, it
is the most desirable above all things" (1 Nephi 11:22).

The fruit that Lehi ate, which made him happy and filled him
with joy, was the love of God. According to Lehi and Nephi there is
nothing better than to experience God's love. I agree. Yes, I have
also eaten this fruit. I have felt God's love for me, and I testify that
Lehi's description is true. To feel the love of God makes you happy
and fills your soul with joy.

That is pretty incredible, isn't it? But, wait. There is something
else to consider. Lehi saw other people trying to make their way to
the tree, but something got in their way. Remember the mist of darkness? Nephi tells us that "the mists of darkness are the temptations
of the devil, which blindeth the eyes, and hardeneth the hearts of the
children of men, and leadeth them away into broad roads, that they
perish and are lost" (1 Nephi 12:17). The adversary is doing everything he can to keep us from eating that fruit. The last thing he wants
for us is happiness and joy. Instead, "he seeketh that all men might
be *miserable* like unto himself" (2 Nephi 2:27; emphasis added).
These mists of darkness are thick today. Again, listen to what
President Benson has said about them:

"The Apostle Paul saw our day. He described it as a time when
such things as blasphemy, dishonesty, cruelty, unnatural affection,
pride and pleasure seeking would abound (see 2 Timothy 3:17). He
also warned that 'evil men and seducers would wax worse and
worse, deceiving and being deceived' (2 Timothy 3:12). Such grim
predictions by prophets of old would be cause for great fear and discouragement if those same prophets had not, at the same time,

offered the solution. In their inspired counsel we can find the answer to the spiritual crises of our age" (*The Teachings of Ezra Taft Benson* [1988], 88).

What is that inspired counsel? What can help us make it through the mists of darkness, so we can arrive safely at the tree and partake of the fruit? Or, in other words, what will help us see through Satan's temptations and make the choices that will help us feel God's love, which makes us happy and brings us joy? The answer is again found in Lehi's dream. He saw something else—something that helped the people find their way through the mist of darkness. It was a "rod of iron, and it extended along the bank of the river, and led to the tree" (1 Nephi 8:19).

Nephi later told his brothers that the rod of iron is "the word of God; and [that] whoso would hearken unto the word of God, and would hold fast unto it, they would never perish; neither could the temptations and the fiery darts of the adversary overpower them unto blindness, to lead them away to destruction" (1 Nephi 15:24).

So, the rod of iron is the word of God—the scriptures. Isn't that incredible? The scriptures can lead you through the mist of darkness and right to the tree. We just need to hold fast to the rod. What does that mean? Simply put, we need to read every day.

Well, now you know that if you read your scriptures daily, they will help you overcome the temptations of Satan and feel God's love. But, what if that's not happening? What if the scriptures aren't doing that for you? What if you just get frustrated the way I used to? Well, first of all, knowing that the result of reading the scriptures is the love of God, which brings us happiness and joy, should help. You now know, if you didn't before, that reading the scriptures is well worth the effort it takes. However, there are some other principles that may help.

First, I believe that it takes effort to achieve good things. Our Father in Heaven expects us to do our part. Think about the example of Oliver Cowdery in his unsuccessful attempts to translate the plates. Explaining why Oliver had failed, the Lord told him, "Behold, you have not understood; you have supposed that I would give it unto you, when you took no thought save it was to ask me" (D&C 9:7). Oliver hadn't done his part. What can we do to do our part?

Well, it sounds simple, but one thing you have to do is read— every day. I have found that it helps me if I set aside a regular time to read my scriptures. For me, the best time is first thing in the morning before I get busy with all the things that fill my day. But you don't have to read in the morning. You could read during lunch or after school or before dinner or in the evening. Just a word of caution here: most of my students who try to read right before they go to bed often find they are so tired that they are only able to read for a couple of minutes. I learned a great lesson about this kind of scripture study while visiting a ward in Canada.

I had flown up to speak and was there over a Sunday. So, I found a local ward I could attend. Being unfamiliar with the area, I got a little lost and arrived late. I found a place in the back of the chapel and took a seat.

The meeting was wonderful. It was a missionary farewell. As usual the family of the departing missionary spoke, and everyone did a great job. The final speaker was the missionary. He was an impressive looking young man, and so I was a little puzzled when he said, "I'm sure a lot of you are surprised to see me here." I was equally taken aback also when everyone seemed to nod yes.

The missionary went on to explain that he had delayed going on his mission because he hadn't felt he had a testimony. When he told his parents that he didn't feel prepared to serve because he didn't have a testimony, his mother had responded by asking if he *wanted* a testimony. Of course he did, and so she suggested he read from the Book of Mormon every day for a week. She also recommended that at the end of the week he put Moroni's promise to the test. This young man went on to say that he had done just what his mother suggested but that nothing happened.

When he told his mother that he didn't feel any differently, she asked him, "When did you read?"

"Before going to bed."

"And how long did you read?" she pressed.

"About five minutes, until I fell asleep."

"How would you feel," his mother had said, "if Heavenly Father only gave you the last five minutes of his day?"

Isn't that a great question? Anyway, then she suggested that he choose another time to read and offered to read with him. They chose to read after he got home from school, and instead of reading for five minutes, they would read for thirty minutes. After one week, the boy was to put Moroni's promise to the test again.

It was here that the young missionary looked down at the pulpit and paused. It was obvious he was trying to gain control of his emotions. When he finally did, he looked up and declared with great feeling that God had answered his prayer. He testified that he knew the Book of Mormon is true and that this is the true Church. He went on to say that he was excited to share his knowledge so that others could be as happy as he had become. He had tasted of the fruit. Isn't it interesting that the thing that made the difference was as simple as scheduling a favorable time to read?

You also probably noticed from that experience that he increased the time he read. Think about it; is five minutes long enough to spend with someone you love? Consider what President Howard W. Hunter encouraged us to do in this regard:

"Those who delve into the scriptural library . . . find that to understand requires more than casual reading or perusal—there must be concentrated study. It is certain that one who studies the scriptures every day accomplishes far more than one who devotes considerable time one day and then lets days go by before continuing. Not only should we study each day, but there should be a regular time set aside when we can concentrate without interference. . . .

"It would be ideal if an hour could be spent each day; but if that much cannot be had, a half hour on a regular basis would result in substantial accomplishment. A quarter of an hour is little time, but it is surprising how much enlightenment and knowledge can be acquired in a subject so meaningful. The important thing is to allow nothing else to ever interfere with our study" (*The Teachings of Howard W. Hunter* [1997], 52–53).

So, according to President Hunter, we need to devote at least fifteen minutes a day or more. Remember, at first that might not be easy. However, as you continue and partake more and more of God's love you will find that even an hour is sometimes not enough.

There is something else that I have found helpful. This principle comes from Doctrine and Covenants 33:16, which reads: "And the Book of Mormon and the holy scriptures are given of me for your instruction; and the power of my Spirit quickeneth all things."

Did you catch that last part? *The Spirit quickens all things.* Now be careful, the word *quicken* doesn't mean to make it go fast, although I admit when you read the scriptures with the Spirit the time does seem to fly. *Quicken* means to "make alive." That's right, when you read with the Spirit, the scriptures come alive. Have you ever felt that something you were reading was written just for you? Many times when I am reading I feel almost as though Heavenly Father and the Savior are speaking directly to me. Let me give you an example.

Early in my career as a seminary teacher, I was offered another job. It was something that I really wanted to do, but taking the job would mean that I would have to stop teaching seminary, which I also loved doing. For weeks I wrestled with the decision. Finally, after much thought and prayer and fasting, I read the following verse: "And now, as ye have begun to teach the word even so I would that ye should continue to teach; and I would that ye would be diligent and temperate in all things" (Alma 38:10).

This was advice Alma gave specifically to his son Shiblon, but when I read the passage, I felt it was for my benefit. That morning the scriptures came alive for me, and I knew that the Lord wanted me to continue teaching seminary.

Now, sometimes it may not be the exact wording, but the feeling we get as we read that makes the scriptures come alive. One young woman I knew related the following experience. It seems that one Friday afternoon her mom informed her that the young woman's uncle had passed away. The young woman didn't know her uncle that well, and so she wasn't too upset. However, she began to think about death and how temporary her life is, and this began to bother her.

That night she had arranged to go out with her friends and was anxious to talk to them about her feelings. Unfortunately, her friends showed little interest in the topic. She found herself in a somber mood and finally asked them to just take her home. By then she was feeling really confused and even a little scared.

After getting home, she went into her bedroom where she noticed her scriptures lying on her nightstand. She opened them, sat down on her bed, and began to read. As she related the experience, she said she couldn't remember exactly what she read. However, as she read, she had the most peaceful feeling come over her, and she knew that everything was okay. She knew that death was a part of God's plan and that he loved her.

That's the kind of thing that can and should happen when you read with the Spirit. Consider what Elder Dallin H. Oaks said concerning this: "Scripture reading may also lead to current revelation on whatever else the Lord wishes to communicate to the reader at that time. We do not overstate the point when we say that the scriptures can be a Urim and Thummim to assist each of us to receive personal revelation.

"Because we believe that scripture reading can help us receive revelation, we are encouraged to read the scriptures again and again. By this means, we obtain access to what our Heavenly Father would have us know and do in our personal lives today. That is one reason Latter-day Saints believe in *daily* scripture study" (*Ensign,* January 1995, 8; emphasis in original).

Just to recap, when you read under the influence of the Spirit, the scriptures can come alive, and you can receive revelation directed to you. So, what can you do to invite the Spirit to be with you when you read? There are lots of things. I will suggest just two.

First of all, I have found it very helpful to *pray* before I read the scriptures. In that prayer I usually ask for the Spirit to be with me as I read. In addition, I make sure to thank my Father in Heaven for the blessing of having the scriptures. Also, if there is anything that I am currently struggling with, I ask for guidance and direction.

Second, I have also found it useful to *ponder* what I read. President Marion G. Romney taught this concerning pondering: "As I have read the scriptures, I have been challenged by the word *ponder,* so frequently used in the Book of Mormon. The dictionary says that *ponder* means 'to weigh mentally, think deeply about, deliberate, meditate.' . . .

"*Pondering* is, in my feeling, a form of prayer. It has, at least, been an approach to the Spirit of the Lord on many occasions" (In Conference Report, April 1973, 117; emphasis in original).

Pondering really pays off, but it is not easy. It takes real effort. Elder Jeffrey R. Holland taught: "Reading which will give you any return on your investment will be an exercise . . . in which your mental and spiritual muscles are stretched and strengthened forever. . . . To ponder [the scriptures] suggests a slow and deliberate examination: indeed, there is no way to read the scriptures whimsically or superficially or quickly. They demand time, prayer, and honest meditation" (*Ensign,* September 1976, 7).

Don't just read the words. Instead, consider deeply what the words *mean.* You can do this by asking questions. For example, Why didn't Nephi murmur like his brothers? or Why were the stripling warriors not killed when all around them men were dying? or how about, What did Joseph Smith do to get an answer to his prayers? One of the best questions you can ask is, How does this apply to me? Nephi called this "liken[ing]" the scriptures to ourselves (1 Nephi 19:23). As you read, the Spirit will lead you through the mists of darkness that surround us in this world (see 2 Nephi 32:5). When you ponder, you are really "feast[ing]" on the word (2 Nephi 32:3). You are satisfying that spiritual hunger you may not have realized you had.

Let me tie this all together with a personal note. My wife, Nancy, and I just had the opportunity of adopting a beautiful little boy. We have been unable to have children for several years, so you can imagine how excited we are. I can't even begin to tell you all the miracles that took place to bring this little boy into our hearts and home. Now, I know there will come a day when my son will have some questions about how he became a part of our family. It may even be a bit confusing for him. To help him, I have written down some things concerning how he came into our lives. One day he will be able to read how his dad felt the first time he saw him, how his father knew from the beginning that he was meant to be a member of this family, and especially how much his dad loves him.

In a very real way our Father in Heaven has done a similar thing for us. He knew that this life would not be easy. He also knew that we would have questions. So, he has given us the scriptures to answer those questions and to assure us that he loves us.

I love the scriptures, and I know you will come to love them, too, as you experience the happiness and joy that result from reading them daily under the influence of the Holy Spirit.

R. Scott Simmons served a mission to Cleveland, Ohio, then attended Brigham Young University and worked at the Missionary Training Center. He has taught seminary and has been an instructor in the Department of Church History and Doctrine at BYU. Currently, he is CES coordinator in Austin, Texas. Scott married Nancy Wright in the Jordan River Utah Temple in 1992. They are the proud parents of a little boy named Matthew. Scott's favorite things to do include teaching, studying Church history, going on outdoor adventures, and spending time with his wife and son.

JOSEPH SMITH, THE RESTORATION, AND YOU

Scott Anderson

One early winter day, the doorway of my office was filled up almost completely by one of my students—a member of the high school football team. He looked somewhat bewildered, so I asked if there was anything I could do to help. He admitted that there was. The girl's choice dance was coming up. His bewilderment was due to the fact that he had not yet been asked. "Who would they want to ask if they don't want to ask me?" he questioned. I told him that girls like humble guys like him, so I couldn't understand it either. He informed me that he and his friends really did want to know what the girls are looking for in a guy.

"So, why don't you just ask them?" I thought this would work quite well. "They might not tell us the whole truth, Brother Anderson. Why don't you ask them?" I could see his point and agreed to run an informal survey to find out what the young women were looking for in an ideal date.

A brief survey was typed to be delivered to about four hundred LDS high-school-age young women. The title of the survey was "Your Perfect Man." The first question was, "How tall should he be?" The answers ranged from 5 feet 2 inches to 6 feet 10 inches. All the young men seemed to feel okay about that since they were all in the general range. The next question was, "How much should he weigh?"

It was evident that some young women are unaware that a young man usually weighs more than a young woman does, even if they are the same height. For example, one answer said the perfect man was to be 6 feet tall, be "muscle-bound," and weigh 125 pounds! It was easy to see that we might have a few problems with the survey.

The next question was about neck size. Why would we ask neck size? Well, it was wrestling season, and as a young man works out on the mat, his neck starts to grow in size. A typical neck size might be 15 to 17 inches. One young lady said a 3-inch neck size would be preferable. I'm not sure, but I think that would be only the size of an esophagus and that's all. One young lady wrote, "I don't care just as long as he does" (we'll talk about that one another day).

Next, we wanted to see if the young women wanted their ideal man to be rippling with muscles, so we asked about performance in a highly publicized exercise in our school—the bench press. The survey simply said, "Bench-press ____ pounds." The young women were to fill in the blank. Young men can generally lift about the same as they weigh, then after conditioning and practice they are able to lift quite a bit more. Like the "400 Club" at BYU whose members can bench-press 400 pounds and could probably change the tire on a small car by picking up the car and taking off the wheel with their bare hands. Anyway, one young woman said that her ideal man would be able to bench-press about 25 pounds—which made all of us feel better about our abilities. One girl said she didn't care how many pounds, just as long as he did all the laundry. (We were to find out that she thought "bench-pressing" was a type of ironing, and she didn't care how many pounds it was—just do all of it!)

As we read through the surveys, it became obvious that some of the answers weren't relevant. But we got an overall picture of what the girls were looking for in the "perfect date." He would combine the physical attributes of Gaston, in the movie *Beauty and the Beast* and possess the character traits of the beast after he had returned to being the prince. The ideal date would therefore be approximately the size of a barge, yet be unfailingly humble, thoughtful, kind, considerate, polite, respectful, and gentle.

As I shared the results of the survey with the young men, they struggled a bit to understand how they could be both "strong" and "gentle," both "macho" and "humble"—and somehow keep it all in balance. We talked about Joseph Smith who is an example of a man who had achieved such balance. By any measure, the Prophet was an ideal specimen of a man. He was 6 feet 2 inches tall, and in his day that was much taller than the average man. He weighed around 200 pounds and was unusually strong and agile (not to mention handsome). But at the same time, he was kind, thoughtful, and considerate. He was also a very spiritual man and a person of great integrity, one whom the Lord had raised up to open the dispensation of the fulness of times.

In seminary we have the opportunity to study the miraculous story of how the gospel was restored, how the Doctrine and Covenants came about, and the great role the Prophet Joseph Smith played in bringing the truth to the earth again. I have a testimony of his divine foreordination and of his great courage, amazing humility, and endless faith. My prayer for you is that you will come to appreciate his tremendous example of devotion to the truth he loved and taught, and even gave his life for, and that this gratitude for the Prophet Joseph Smith and the Restoration can change your life.

Elder Neal A. Maxwell said, "With the Restoration came a clear understanding of who we are. . . . Isn't it marvelous to ponder how much the Prophet Joseph Smith learned throughout the extended process of restoring the holy priesthood, the holy endowment, the holy sealing power? But young Joseph, whose impact would become global, merely went into the Sacred Grove to find out which local church he should join! How generous God is!" (May 2, 1993, Priesthood Commemoration Fireside at Temple Square).

Because you have been saved to be part of the final dispensation, your potential is unlimited! Elder Maxwell went on to say,

"However, when you and I come to understand our true identities, God loves us too much to let us be content with what we have achieved spiritually up to now, because He is a perfect Father. He knows what we have the power to become, and He has His special ways of being lovingly insistent."

So how do we "come to understand our true identities"? How do we learn to follow the promptings of a loving Father in Heaven as he is being "lovingly insistent" that we become all we can be? With all I know, and with all my heart, I testify to you that as you study the life of the Prophet Joseph Smith and exercise your faith to try with all your might to live the Savior's teachings, you will find the answers to these questions and come to know your part in this— the final gospel dispensation.

Learning to Know Your True Identity

One of the beautiful lessons taught in the First Vision came with the very first word our Heavenly Father spoke as he visited young Joseph. Imagine this young farm boy simply going to a grove to pray and suddenly having such a glorious vision unfolded before him. As the light descended and Joseph gazed into the loving faces of Deity, the first word he heard spoken to him was, "Joseph." Can any of us begin to imagine what it would be like to hear the God of all Creation, even our loving Heavenly Father, call us by name? The very God of Heaven and Earth was that aware of Joseph, one young boy. What a startling realization that the impersonal force for good he had always heard about from other professors of religion was standing before him as a personal, loving, caring Heavenly Father. As soon as Joseph gained his composure, he asked for the direction he had come seeking. And what a marvelous light was restored to the earth from that very moment. How generous God is!

Not only did Joseph Smith learn that he was a child of God and that his Heavenly Father loved and cared for him, he also found out that there was a work for him to do. He began to glimpse what it meant to be here in the last days and to have been saved to do a great work in preparing for the Second Coming.

Are we allowing this light to come into our own lives? Think back on this morning when you looked in the mirror. Did you smile at yourself and say, "Good morning, isn't it great to be me! I just can't wait to have another wonderful day!" Or was it more like, "Good morning, swamp witch! What happened to you overnight?" Maybe you sang your favorite hymn, "When upon life's *pillows* you are tempest-tossed, when you are discouraged, thinking all is lost!" Why does this happen? Is it because we have our morning prayer, "Good morning, Heavenly Father," and he answers, "Good morning, ugly child!" Can you imagine him saying, "Oh, I am sorry. I made a mistake when I created you, but just hang on, and I will correct it in the Resurrection!" Of course not! We know that Heavenly Father doesn't want us to feel that way. However, Nephi warns us that in the last days the adversary will whisper in our ears (see 2 Nephi 28:22) and teach us untruths. So what would happen if tomorrow morning when we heard those discouraging whispers from the wrong source—"You sure have an ugly body!"—we were to let the truth make us free and just say, "Oh, yeah? Well, you don't have a body at all!" Then ignore those lies. Yes, it is true that just as he tried with Joseph Smith, the adversary will try to get us to forget our destiny, put aside what we came here to do, and not allow the Lord's magnificent light to penetrate us. You, too, were saved for this wonderful day and have a glorious mission to fulfill. You were a valiant spirit in the premortal world and have been blessed with a marvelous destiny.

As we come to understand our true identities, our hearts and minds become open to the prompting of the Spirit, and our Father in Heaven can literally direct our actions as he did Joseph's. Joseph Smith learned his own true identity the very second Heavenly Father spoke to him in the Sacred Grove. I know that Heavenly Father knows *you* by name, too. He will give you guidance and direction as you seek it and learn to listen to his Spirit.

Listening to the Spirit

Denice sat quietly in the back of the room. She seemed reluctant to leave. She kept feeling the prompting, and she felt she knew what she needed to do. But could she do it? She knew that Joseph Smith had found the courage to think of his mother's needs, and she understood that Nephi had found the courage, even when his father, Lehi, was murmuring, to go to his father for counsel. But her father was so far away from the Church and so disinterested. However, as she had listened that day in class to the account of the broken bow (see 1 Nephi 16) and listened as Lehi complained against God, and Nephi went to him *anyway,* the Spirit had plainly prompted her to reach out of her comfort zone and try to help her father. She was so busy in school and had so many other things to do, but she knew that in this time of her own great need, she should think of her father and try to find some way to help him.

That night she prayed for strength to talk to her dad about the gospel. She was afraid of how he might respond, but she picked up the phone anyway to call him in Canada. In their conversation, she finally found the courage to try. "Dad, thank you for caring about me so much. I just want you to know how much I love you. You are one of the people I trust deeply in my life. I am learning some wonderful things here at school. Some of them are about the Book of Mormon and the Church, and I would like to share them with you—"

Her father interrupted the conversation. "Denice, you know how I feel about that—let's talk about something else."

"But, Dad, I've always felt that it would be wonderful if I could have a blessing from you, since no one loves me like you do."

"Let's talk about something else!" he snapped. Their brief conversation ended and left her feeling frustrated and empty.

Three months later, after enjoying many more wonderful

experiences with the scriptures, Denice was headed home for Christmas. She called her father the night before she was to leave. In their conversation, she couldn't hold back and once again she asked, "Dad, while I am home for the Christmas break, can I share some of the things I have been learning about the Church?"

"You know how I feel about that," came her father's terse reply. She didn't know what to say. Then the silence was broken by her father's tearful confession. "I'm sorry, Denice, I just can't wait until you get home to tell you. When you talked to me last September, it touched me so deeply, I went to see the bishop the next day. I finished project temple about two weeks ago, and last week I was ordained an elder. I have a present wrapped under the tree that is an offer to give you a father's blessing while you are home. Thank you, Denice. Thank you for wanting so much to share all this with me."

President Gordon B. Hinckley has said, "I have seen miracles in my time, my brothers and sisters. The greatest miracle of all, I believe, is the transformation that comes into the life of a man or a woman who accepts the restored gospel of Jesus Christ and tries to live it in his or her life. How thankful I am for the wonders of the restored gospel of Jesus Christ. It is indeed a marvelous work and a wonder which has been brought to pass by the power of the Almighty in behalf of His sons and daughters" (address delivered at Vacaville/Santa Rosa, California, 21 May 1995).

Just as Joseph Smith was richly rewarded for asking merely to know which local church to join, Denice was also generously blessed for having the courage to listen to the Spirit and ask her father for a blessing. Her life, the life of her father, and the life of her entire family will never be the same.

In February of 1847, when the Prophet Joseph appeared to him in a dream or vision, Brigham asked his predecessor if he had a message for the Brethren. The Prophet said: "Tell the people to be humble and faithful, and be sure to keep the Spirit of the Lord and it will lead them right. Be careful and not turn away the small still voice; it will teach you what to do and where to go; it will yield the fruits of the kingdom. Tell the brethren to keep their hearts open to conviction, so that when the Holy Ghost comes to them, their hearts will be ready to receive it."

The Prophet further directed Brigham Young as follows: "They can tell the Spirit of the Lord from all other spirits; it will whisper peace and joy to their souls; it will take malice, hatred, strife, and all evil from their hearts; and their whole desire will be to do good, bring forth righteousness and build up the kingdom of God" (Manuscript History of Brigham Young, 1846–1847, comp. Elden J. Watson, Salt Lake City [1971], 529).

Church history teaches how the Prophet Joseph Smith's whole desire was to bring forth righteousness and the kingdom of God against all opposition. He states: "From my boyhood until the present time I have been hunted like a roe upon the mountain. I have never been allowed to live like other men. I have been driven, chased, stoned, whipped, robbed, mobbed, imprisoned, persecuted, accused falsely of everything bad" (in John Pulsipher, "Autobiography," typescript, BYU, 7).

One example follows: "Certain residents of Hyrum, Ohio, vented their personal feelings with mob action directed against the Prophet and Sidney Rigdon. Stimulated by whiskey and hidden behind blackened faces, a gang of more than two dozen men dragged Joseph from his bed during the night of March 24, 1832. Choking him into submission, they stripped him naked, scratched his skin with their fingernails, tore his hair, then smeared his body with tar and feathers. A vial of nitric acid forced against his teeth splashed on his face; a front tooth was broken. Meanwhile, other members of the mob dragged Rigdon by his heels from his home, bumping his head on the frozen ground, which left him delirious for days. The Prophet's friends spent the night removing the tar to help him keep a Sunday morning preaching appointment. He addressed a congregation that included Simonds Ryder, organizer of the mob"

(James B. Allen and Glen M. Leonard, *The Story of the Latter-day Saints* [1992], 81).

Faith to Follow the Savior

When I think how the Prophet preached the morning after this attack by the mob, I am overcome with gratitude for this example of "carrying on." Can we even imagine his bruised and welted body, burned and beaten, his face scarred from the night's ordeal, and with all this, he was still able to speak of the joy of the gospel of Jesus Christ. How easily he could have pointed out his enemies sitting amongst them, and then he could have turned his friends against them, but he would not. I am amazed at his forbearance, even with those who despised him. The Prophet Joseph truly followed the Savior in forgiving everyone—even his enemies.

W. W. Phelps, a friend of Joseph and Emma's, joined the Church but later apostatized. While living in Missouri, he and others signed a document that stated falsely that the Saints were in rebellion against the state. This document would come into the hands of Governor Boggs who would then issue the order to either exterminate or drive all Mormons from the state.

There is no way to begin to describe what the Saints went through, in part because of the treachery of Phelps. Joseph was imprisoned for almost six months, Saints were killed, homes were burned, women attacked, the members of the Church were driven a distance of more than 240 miles, across a snow-swept prairie, and Joseph's family was driven from him. After the terrible trek, Emma records arriving at the Mississippi River and seeing it frozen over. The wagons drove across, but because of the fear of the ice breaking, she went upstream and braved her way by foot across the ice with a child hanging on each leg, a baby in each arm, and pages of the inspired version of the Bible sewn into her petticoats for protection. She knew if the ice broke, she and the children would be swept away to their deaths. Following their expulsion from Missouri, the

Saints would be forced to live in a malaria-infested swamp, and so many would become very ill. As a result of W. W. Phelps's betrayal and the actions of others, untold suffering had come on Joseph and the members of the Church.

Some time later, after the most difficult persecution was past and the swamp had been drained and the city of Nauvoo was being built, W. W. Phelps wrote to Joseph to ask forgiveness for what he had done and to request permission to return to the Church and the friendship of the Saints. Joseph replied: "You may in some measure realize what my feelings, as well as Elder Rigdon's and Brother Hyrum's were, when we read your letter—truly our hearts were melted into tenderness and compassion when we ascertained your resolves . . .

"Believing your confession to be real, and your repentance genuine, I shall be happy once again to give you the right hand of fellowship, and rejoice over the returning prodigal.

"Your letter was read to the Saints last Sunday, and an expression of their feeling was taken when it was unanimously *resolved, That* W. W. Phelps should be received into fellowship.

"'Come on, dear brother, since the war is past, For friends at first, are friends again at last.'

"Yours as ever,

"Joseph Smith Jun." (*History of the Church,* 4:163–64).

W. W. Phelps later wrote the hymn "Praise to the Man" as a tribute to Joseph Smith and was one of the principal speakers at the Prophet's funeral, where he stood and wept as he described the forgiveness he had been granted by this great prophet of God.

Joseph learned to follow the Spirit with exactness. For his love of the Savior and his sacrifice for the gospel, Joseph Smith deserves all the "praise" we can give him. There is no greater tribute given any other mortal man than that recorded in section 135 of the Doctrine and Covenants, where it says, "Joseph Smith, the Prophet and Seer of the Lord, has done more, save Jesus only, for the salvation of men in this world, than any other man that ever lived in it" (v. 3).

As Joseph was approaching the Martyrdom, he again reminds us of those things that matter most. The morning he left Nauvoo for Carthage, he returned home three times to hug his children, hold his wife, and express his love to them. He loved his children and was a great father. He adored his wife and was an excellent husband. He cared so deeply for his mother and father and brothers and sisters. I have admired young people I have known who have followed Joseph's example in this regard.

I once watched a young woman, who was leaving with her boyfriend to go to a movie, return to the house to invite her little brother to come along. How loved and important he must have felt as he enjoyed that evening with the couple. I have felt the power of a wonderful son, who when he was young, started the tradition of hugging everyone in the family "good night." As he was dropped off at the MTC and his happy but somewhat lonely parents returned home and prepared for bed, his mother quietly said, "I am going to miss that big boy's hug tonight," only to turn down the covers and find a note pinned on the pillows that said, "Here is your hug for tonight!" Thank you, wonderful youth, for the love you show your families.

So why was Joseph like this, and why are there youth today who are such examples of great love? The answer is that they all have the same hero, Jesus Christ. He, the Perfect Man, provided the greatest example of love ever known. Not that long ago, really, he left that upper room with his disciples after they had sung a hymn. He left all but three disciples outside the Garden. The three came in, and he asked for their prayers. He went a little way off and fell on his face, enduring a type of spiritual suffering and agony so intense that there is no way to express it. Those drops of blood, which came from every pore, were shed for you and me. He didn't need to atone for himself. He was perfect. And so, it was an act of perfect selflessness. He could have stopped at any moment. The suffering would have ended any mortal's life, but he would not yet die, for his work was not complete.

Think of it. Hours of suffering, then the betrayal by a trusted friend, being mocked, spit upon, scourged, belittled, and tortured by a crown of cruel thorns. He could have ended any or all of it at any moment, yet he went on to endure the horrors of crucifixion, with the awful spikes and wrenching pain. How unbelievable is it that he would plead in behalf of his tormentors, "Father, forgive them; for they know not what they do"? (Luke 23:34). Consider the hours, the pain, and then the loneliness: "My God, my God, why hast thou forsaken me?" (Matthew 27:46). Would the Atonement have been complete without the Savior experiencing the spiritual loneliness we feel when we sin—when the Spirit leaves us because we are not worthy of it? He, though sinless, hung alone as all heaven wept. He knows spiritual loneliness, and he will be there for us so that we need never be alone. Finally, when it was complete, his great heart burst, and his immortal spirit left his body. He left this life with a heart broken for us. I love him so much. I know he lives. He is our Hero. He is the Perfect Man.

Scott Anderson served a mission to South Germany, and then married Angelle Clark in the Salt Lake Temple. They are the parents of seven children and grandparents of eleven—nine of them boys. Brother Anderson has a Ph.D. in Marriage and Family Therapy from BYU. He has taught for thirty years in the Church Education System, and is a faculty member at the Orem Institute of Religion adjacent to Utah Valley State College. Brother Anderson enjoys home construction projects, writing, running, and making memories with his family. He loves to teach and share his love of the Savior and His gospel. He has been involved in the "Especially for Youth" Program since it began. He and his wife have enjoyed serving as missionary companions in their ward in Bluffdale, Utah.

ALWAYS

Lisa Heckmann Olsen

Years ago I stood in front of a wiggly group of Primary children. They were not paying attention to my carefully planned and rehearsed sharing time lesson, and so I asked the children to try something new with me. I turned to a large picture of Christ and asked them to think about Jesus for one minute. As I followed the second hand on my watch, the room went silent. Heads, one by one, were quietly bowed. The Spirit filled our little Primary room. It had actually changed their behavior. I quietly asked the children to share a story they had remembered as they were thinking about Jesus. One child mentioned that he knew he was loved because "Jesus loves the children." Another child said that Jesus died on the cross for her. As their teacher, I was grateful that these children knew Christ and could feel his Spirit. It was an unforgettable teaching moment, like that described in Doctrine and Covenants 50:22. "Wherefore, he that preacheth and he that receiveth, understand one another, and both are edified and rejoice together."

I explained to the children that our experience was over and it was time to go to class. I thanked them for being so reverent. A four-year-old Sunbeam, clearly frustrated, raised her hand and asked, "Sister Olsen, is it okay if I think about Jesus all of the time?" Her concern was sincere. I assured her that always thinking of Jesus would be *his* greatest wish. I will never forget the lesson she brought to my remembrance: to think about Jesus all of the time.

The Book of Mormon prophet Alma always remembered Christ. Do you recall Alma's dramatic and powerful first appearance in the Book of Mormon? He was one of the priests in wicked king Noah's court. He had been present on several occasions in which the prophet Abinadi had called the king and his people to repentance. Alma had caught a spark of the gospel light that Abinadi was working so hard to ignite. When king Noah condemned Abinadi to death by fire, Alma pleaded for Abinadi's life. He knew in his heart that the testimony Abinadi bore was true. "But the king was more wroth, and caused that Alma should be cast out from among them, and sent his servants after him that they might slay him" (Mosiah 17:3). The king's command, however, backfired, and Alma fled from the servants.

"Now, there was in Mormon a fountain of pure water, and Alma resorted thither, there being near the water a thicket of small trees, where he did hide himself in the daytime from the searches of the king" (Mosiah 18:5). The word spread among the believers in the land that Alma was teaching and baptizing. In a powerful passage of scripture, Alma invited the believers to be baptized: "Behold, here are the waters of Mormon (for thus were they called) and now, as ye are desirous to come into the fold of God, and to be called his people, and are willing to bear one another's burdens, that they may be light; Yea, and are willing to mourn with those that mourn; yea, and comfort those that stand in need of comfort, and to stand as witnesses of God at all times and in all things, and in all places that ye may be in, even until death, that ye may be redeemed of God, and be numbered with those of the first resurrection, that ye may have eternal life" (Mosiah 18:8–9).

To stand as a witness of God is evidence that we always remember Christ.

At All Times

My maiden name will always be Heckmann. Like Nephi, I was "born of goodly parents" (1 Nephi 1:1), who had equally wonderful parents, my grandparents. I loved visiting Grandpa Heckmann's fruit farm in Providence, Utah. I vividly remember passing out ice cream to the fruit pickers, helping my grandpa weigh cherries, hanging upside down on the swing set, exploring the run-down chicken coop, making bread with my grandma, sleeping in the sunken-in "yellow bed," and many other choice memories. My grandpa was a hard worker, one who watched Lawrence Welk while eating a TV dinner, who loved cookies and ice cream, and who lovingly cared for my grandmother during her illness. My favorite store in Providence was Tires, a small, family-owned grocery store. Once I was short a little change to buy a treat. The clerk simply asked, "Are you Will Heckmann's grandchild?" "Yes," was my proud response. "Go ahead and take the treat. Will is good for the rest!" The best gift that my grandpa ever gave me was his name. It is a name associated with honor, respect, and dignity. I am proud to be a Heckmann.

When I married, I added a new name: Olsen. I have come to love all the Olsens. I now represent this family and have the power to cause this honorable name to be respected or disrespected.

At baptism we receive the name of Christ, which is as important, if not more so, than our own surname. Read the following verses of scripture that focus on the name of Christ:

"That they are willing to take upon them the name of thy Son" (D&C 20:77).

"That ye are willing to take upon you the name of Christ, by baptism—yea, by following your Lord and your Savior down into the water" (2 Nephi 31:13).

"Yea, blessed is this people who are willing to bear my name; for in my name shall they be called; and they are mine" (Mosiah 26:18).

"Have they not read the scriptures, which say ye must take

upon you the name of Christ, which is my name? For by this name shall ye be called at the last day" (3 Nephi 27:5).

Taking upon us the name of Christ is an act of association with honor, respect, dignity, and truth. We covenant to honor his name always. We never get a break or have time off. It is a twenty-four-hour-a-day covenant.

Picture this. You are traveling on a long, deserted stretch of highway. In the distance you observe a car speeding recklessly. The car crosses the median. Suddenly the car jerks in the opposite direction. The driver has attempted to correct his mistake, but as a result of the impulsive action, the car rolls and comes to a screeching halt. As you pass the scene, it is obvious that the driver is injured. Did I mention that you are a doctor with a cell phone? What do you do? It seems absurd that you would continue to drive, pretending the accident didn't happen. Just because you are not at the hospital or the office in your doctor's uniform with your official badge pinned on does not change the fact that you have lifesaving knowledge. You would stop to offer help until the ambulance arrives.

We don't have to be at church, or at Young Men or Young Women activities, or seminary, or wearing a missionary badge to be a witness. Our actions should always reflect the name of Christ. When the resurrected Savior visited the Nephites, he commanded them to "let your light so shine before this people, that they may see your good works and glorify your Father who is in heaven" (3 Nephi 12:16).

In All Things

In 1990 the First Presidency issued a pamphlet to the youth of the Church. *For the Strength of Youth* warns, "You are at a critical time in your lives. This is a time for you not only to live righteously but also to set an example for your peers" (Salt Lake City: The Church of Jesus Christ of Latter-day Saints, 1990, 3). At this "critical time," it is important that, like Alma, you live righteously and stand as a witness in "all things." *For the Strength of Youth* asks you to consider the ways in which you can stand as a witness in your dating, dress and appearance, friendshipping, honesty, language, media choices, mental and physical health, music and dancing, sexual purity, Sunday behavior, and service. All youth will face these issues at some point in their growing-up years. Likewise, there will be a great need for spiritual help and repentance. The First Presidency knows this and uses the pamphlet to help you understand that. They conclude the pamphlet by discussing worthiness and service. I invite you to carefully and prayerfully review *For the Strength of Youth.* You will never outgrow its guidelines and standards. They will teach you how to stand up!

I have a favorite former student who had the courage to stand up in a public situation. She sat at a table with her friends, three girls and two boys. As they worked on an art project, the conversation turned to recently viewed movies. They began to talk about a movie with "incredible computer graphics." They were impressed with the morphing and realistic interpretation of obvious fantasy. The movie was rated R. She sat quietly for awhile until one of the boys asked, "Did you like the movie?" She looked him squarely in the eye and said confidently, "I didn't see the movie." (The Spirit brings confidence—what a great feeling! You have the Spirit when you're choosing the right!)

"WHAT?" was the shocked response, "EVERYONE has seen (name of the movie)!"

The boy was baffled and totally unprepared for her next unsolicited statement: "I have never seen an R-rated movie!"

The entire group almost fell out of their chairs. "NEVER?" they asked unbelieving.

"Never," she returned.

One girl hollered across the classroom, "She has never seen an R-rated movie!"

The girl sat with a smile on her face, not embarrassed in the least. Other doubting students swarmed to the table to continue the interrogation. She patiently answered their questions. The conversation turned positive as students one by one expressed regret for the movies they had seen. Many committed to follow her example.

Standing as a witness in all things does not always have to happen in public. It can happen in other, more subtle ways. I have a nephew, Alma, who just turned one. In his baby blessing, his father, Jim, pronounced that Alma would be a "friend to the friendless." This little boy already has a smile that could melt any heart. It is easy to see that this is one of his gifts. He will be able to reach out to others. Isn't that exactly what Christ did? He was always a friend to the friendless.

I believe that every teenager at one time or another has felt as if he has no friends and that no one cares. It may be our witness of Christ's love that helps others change this feeling of insecurity. The way we treat others can have either a positive or a negative effect.

I've learned a lot from my art students. Camille (name changed) had an impact on a socially struggling student, Mac (name changed). It was obvious that Mac was different from the other students. His clothes were unkempt, his hair was a mess, and he had odd mannerisms. As a teacher, I struggled when Mac would make comments out loud that had nothing to do with the subject at hand. It was an obvious cry for attention and help. He struggled just to have conversations with others. He sat at the back of the classroom, alone. However, Mac was a talented artist, a gift passed down from his mother.

One day he approached me at the same time as Camille. Camille was beautiful and also kind. Both wanted feedback on their printmaking project. Mac was first, and I had no suggestions for improvement—his print was beautiful. Apparently Camille felt the same way. She reached for Mac's hand and said, "Mac, your print is beautiful! It's the best one in the class!" He couldn't even look her in the face. Instead he just melted. It didn't end with that compliment. She yelled across the room to a friend, "Come and see Mac's print—

it's awesome!" From the moment of her speaking up, Mac was established as the best artist in the class. Mac slowly integrated himself back into the classroom, and Camille continued to be friendly and compliment him. She made the difference.

In All Places

A few years ago our little family had a stopover in Mesquite, Nevada. We stayed in a family hotel but went to eat at an "all you can eat" breakfast buffet. Getting to the buffet was complicated and involved navigating through endless concourses of slot machines. Cole, who was then three, sensed something different. We proceeded to the buffet and loaded our plates with our favorite high-calorie, high-fat breakfast foods. Cole's plate was filled with pancakes and "chicken" (bacon). I assumed that he would quickly dig in. He didn't. His little spirit was upset and agitated. As we started to eat, Cole stood up in his seat and sang, "Follow the prophet, follow the prophet, Follow the prophet; don't go astray!" (*Children's Songbook*, 110). It was difficult to make him stop singing. I was embarrassed and proud at the same time. Embarrassed because he was singing loudly and causing a scene, but proud because he had to let everyone know what he felt. I wondered if anyone understood what he sang and if it actually made someone think.

The scriptures are filled with examples of witnesses in all places. Some witnessed in their home (Nephi), some with friends (Alma the Younger), and others at the end of their lives (Mormon). In some places they feared for their own lives. Abinadi was such a prophet. Abinadi testified of Christ and exposed many of the people's iniquities. They were not happy with him. "Now it came to pass that when Abinadi had spoken these words unto them they were wroth with him, and sought to take away his life; but the Lord delivered him out of their hands." When King Noah heard the words of Abinadi, he said, "I command you to bring Abinadi hither, that I may slay him, for he has said these things that he might stir up my people to anger one with another, and to raise contentions among my people; therefore I will slay him" (Mosiah 11:26, 28).

King Noah was angry, not only because Abinadi exposed his sins, but because he also prophesied his death. Abinadi spent time among the people in disguise for two years. He continued to teach and to prophesy. The people were angered and took him forcefully to the king. He was sent to prison until the priests could gather for a council. Once convened, "they began to question him, that they might cross him, that thereby they might have wherewith to accuse him; but he answered them boldly, and withstood all their questions, yea, to their astonishment; for he did withstand them in all their questions, and did confound them in all their words" (Mosiah 12:19). The king commanded his priests to take Abinadi away because "he is mad" (Mosiah 13:1). However, they were unable to put their hands on him because of divine intervention.

Abinadi's final message included the Ten Commandments and a powerful testimony of the Savior. Once again Noah commanded the priests to take Abinadi away and put him to death. But his testimony was so powerful that it affected Alma. Alma pleaded for Abinadi's life. Even so, Abinadi suffered death by fire. In the face of death, he stood as a witness to the end. Do you ever wonder if Abinadi felt like a successful missionary? I wonder if he was discouraged because the priests and the king didn't listen. But one did. That one soul became a prophet.

It is unlikely we will ever face a situation like Abinadi's. But we might someday find ourselves in an unusual place with an opportunity to testify of the Savior.

In 1989 my parents had an amazing adventure. My father had been invited to communist Russia to perform some scientific research. They stayed in the country for six months, living like ordinary Russian citizens. They had no special privileges. When they were briefed on the trip, they were advised never to proselyte. However, if someone approached them and asked about their beliefs, they were told they could speak freely, but only as long as they were asked questions. In accordance with the law, they took with them one Russian Book of Mormon, just in case someone asked.

Everything about my parents—their dress, their actions, their speech—had to reflect the gospel of Jesus Christ. They carried with them the hope that someone would ask them about their beliefs. While in Moscow a young scientist quizzed my parents. He wanted to know about their religion. They testified of Christ and his gospel here on earth. Then they presented to him their one Russian Book of Mormon. He took the book and held it to his chest. He had never owned scriptures before. With tears, he thanked them for the gift. He opened the book, read a passage, and said, "Such a beautiful book, such perfect Russian." He repeated over and over, "Such a beautiful book." He complimented my parents, who were not the first Americans he knew. "You are different. You have a peculiar energy about you." To their surprise he pulled out a key and opened a locked desk drawer. He carefully placed the Book of Mormon inside. Their gift was precious. He then surprised them with the old Russian bow of deep respect: he stood up, raised his hand, bent halfway over, and swept the ground with his right hand. They were astonished.

Alma is specific about the gift we receive when we stand as a witness of God. It is the most valuable gift we could possibly receive here on earth: the Spirit of God. "Serve him and keep his commandments, that he may pour out his Spirit more abundantly upon you" (Mosiah 18:10). Each week, when we renew our baptismal covenants through the sacrament, we receive the same promise that Alma spoke of at the waters of Mormon. We witness unto God that we "are willing to take upon [us] the name of thy Son, and always remember him and keep his commandments which he has given [us]; that [we] may always have his Spirit to be with [us]. Amen" (D&C 20:77). It is a perfect cycle: when we stand as a witness of Christ, we are blessed with his Spirit. Then, in turn, his Spirit will give us courage, strength, and inspiration to become a more perfect witness.

May you remember the promise that you made at baptism: a covenant to stand as a witness of God "at all times and in all things, and in all places." Each week while taking the sacrament, I hope that you will be filled with hope, courage, and renewed strength to continue the good work. Always take hope in the words of our prophet, President Gordon B. Hinckley, who loves you: "I believe we have the finest generation of young people that this Church has ever known. They are better educated; they are better motivated; they know the scriptures; they live the Word of Wisdom; they pay their tithing; they pray. They try to do the right thing. They are bright and able, clean and fresh, attractive and smart. These are very substantial in number. More of them go on missions than ever before. More of them marry in the temple. They know what the gospel is about, and they are trying to live it, looking to the Lord for His guidance and help" ("Your Greatest Challenge, Mother," *Ensign,* November 2000, 97–98). The Lord loves his children, and our Savior needs us to testify of his perfect life and example. May your example reflect his life always.

Lisa Heckmann Olsen married Brent Olsen in the Manti Utah Temple. They are the proud parents of Cole, Sierra, and Maya. After serving a mission in Geneva, Switzerland, Lisa taught French at the Missionary Training Center in Provo. She graduated from Brigham Young University with a degree in art and French education. Lisa taught art at Timpview High School in Utah for ten years. She started working for EFY as a counselor in 1983. She loves painting, drawing, making art projects with her children, traveling, gardening, cooking, serving as a Laurel advisor, and being home. She and her family reside in American Fork, Utah.

16

YOUTH OF THE NOBLE BIRTHRIGHT

Ron Bartholomew

On many occasions, President Gordon B. Hinckley has said: "You are youth of the noble birthright. . . . "You are great young people. I have said again and again, we have the finest generation of young people ever in the history of this Church. . . . You are intrinsically better. You are wonderful young people!" (*Teachings of Gordon B. Hinckley* [Salt Lake City: Deseret Book, 1997], 711, 714). He also said, "You represent a great generation in the history of the world and in the history of this Church. In terms of the Church, I feel that you are part of the greatest generation we have ever had" ("True to the Faith," Salt Lake Valley-Wide Institute Fireside, January 21, 1996). You have heard it many times—chosen generation—youth of the noble birthright. Exactly what does that mean? Let's answer this question by explaining: (1) *when* you were chosen, (2) *why* you were chosen, (3) for *what purpose* you were chosen, and (4) *how* you can fulfill your part of Heavenly Father's plan for you while you are on this earth.

When Were You Chosen?

We are all Heavenly Father's spirit children, and we lived with him in the premortal life, before we were born. The Apostle Paul taught that during our premortal lives, the Lord assigned each of us a specific time and place to come and live on this earth: The Lord "hath made of one blood all nations of men for to dwell on all the face of the earth, and hath determined the times before appointed, and the bounds of their habitation" (Acts 17:26). These two assignments—*where* we would live and *when* we would live—were part of the "foreordination," or the "ordination" we received before we were born.

Elder Bruce R. McConkie further explained that in addition to a specific time and place, "the *race and nation* in which men are born in this world is a direct result of their pre-existent life. All the spirit hosts of heaven deemed worthy to receive mortal bodies were foreordained to pass through this earthly probation in the particular *race and nation* suited to their needs, circumstances, and talents" (*Mormon Doctrine,* 2d ed. [Salt Lake City: Bookcraft, 1966], 616; emphasis added).

Why Were You Chosen for This Time and Station?

The gift of agency began in the premortal life. Because every spirit used its agency differently there, some became more faithful to Heavenly Father than others. President Joseph Fielding Smith explained: "God gave his children their free agency even in the spirit world, by which the individual spirits had the privilege, just as men have here, of choosing the good and rejecting the evil, or partaking of the evil to suffer the consequences of their sins. Because of this, some even there were more faithful than others in keeping the commandments of the Lord. . . .

" . . . The spirits of men were not equal. They may have had an equal start [see Alma 13:5–7], and we know they were all innocent in the beginning; but the right of free agency which was given to them enabled some to outstrip others, and thus, through the eons of immortal existence, to become more intelligent, more faithful, for they were free to act for themselves, to think for themselves, to receive the truth or rebel against it" (*Doctrines of Salvation,* comp. Bruce R.

McConkie, 3 vols. [Salt Lake City: Bookcraft, 1954–56], 1:58–59). We know that Jesus became the most righteous of any spirit in the pre-earth life through his constant righteous use of agency there. We also know that every spirit chose to follow either Heavenly Father or Satan. You are here *now* because of your faithfulness *then*.

The Lord explained to Abraham that among those who followed Heavenly Father, some were so exceptionally faithful they were chosen to be his spiritual leaders here on earth. Abraham records: "Among all these there were many of the noble and great ones; and God saw these souls that they were good, and he stood in the midst of them, and he said: These I will make my rulers; for he stood among those that were spirits, and he saw that they were good; and he said unto me: Abraham, thou art one of them; thou wast chosen before thou wast born" (Abraham 3:22–23). In other words, because they were "noble," "great," and "good," some were chosen in the world of spirits to be "rulers," or spiritual leaders here on earth.

You are part of that chosen or select group of "noble and great" spirits. According to President Ezra Taft Benson, "For nearly six thousand years, God has held you in reserve to make your appearance in the final days before the Second Coming of the Lord. . . . While our generation will be comparable in wickedness to the days of Noah, when the Lord cleansed the earth by flood, there is a major difference this time. It is that God has saved for the final inning some of his strongest children, who will help bear off the Kingdom triumphantly. And that is where you come in, for you are the generation that must be prepared to meet your God.

"All through the ages the prophets have looked down through the corridors of time to our day. Billions of the deceased and those yet to be born have their eyes on us. Make no mistake about it—you are a marked generation" ("In His Steps," in *Speeches of the Year, 1979* [Provo: Brigham Young University Press, 1980], 59).

You are part of this "marked generation"!

In order for you to accomplish this special mission, you needed to be born into a situation where you would have access to the restored gospel of Jesus Christ. Moses taught that this was also part of your premortal foreordination. He said that among all of Heavenly Father's spirit children, the most faithful were chosen to come forth as members of the royal, chosen family lineage of Jacob (Israel): "When the most High . . . separated the sons of Adam, he set the bounds of the people according to the number of the children of Israel" (Deuteronomy 32:8). Elder Melvin J. Ballard wrote that being born into this family is an additional reward for faithfulness in the premortal life: "There was a group of souls tested, tried, and proven before they were born into the world, and the Lord provided a lineage for them. That lineage is the house of Israel, the lineage of Abraham, Isaac and Jacob and their posterity. Through this lineage were to come the true and tried souls that had demonstrated their righteousness in the spirit world before they came here" (*Melvin J. Ballard—Crusader for Righteousness* [Salt Lake City: Bookcraft, 1966], 218–19).

When you receive your patriarchal blessing (the word patriarchal means "father," so this is a father's blessing from your Heavenly Father), the Lord tells you from which of Jacob's sons you have descended. This is of utmost importance, because Jacob was Isaac's son, and Isaac was the son of Abraham. Abraham was so faithful that the Lord promised him that all who ever received the gospel and the blessings of the priesthood would either be born into his family line through his son Isaac and his grandson Jacob or adopted into it (see Abraham 2:9–11; Genesis 17:19–21; 28:13–15).

Elder Bruce R. McConkie explained the great spiritual advantage it is to you to be born into this chosen family line: "To bring to pass the salvation of the greatest possible number of his spirit children the Lord, in general, sends the most righteous and worthy spirits to earth through the lineage of Abraham and Jacob. . . .

" . . . Those so grouped together during their mortal probation have more abundant opportunities to make and keep the covenants of salvation" (*Mormon Doctrine,* 216).

Because you were chosen in the premortal life to be born into the family of Abraham, you now have the opportunity to enjoy the blessings of the gospel, all the ordinances of the priesthood, and ultimately eternal life. Have you ever wondered why you were so fortunate to be born here and now, where you are able to accept and enjoy the blessings of the gospel? It is because of your faithfulness in the premortal life!

President Harold B. Lee testified of this when he said: "You are now born into a family to which you have come, into the nations through which you have come, as a reward for the kind of lives you lived before you came here. . . .

"All these rewards were seemingly promised, or foreordained, before the world was. Surely these matters must have been determined by the kind of lives we had lived in that premortal spirit world. Some may question these assumptions, but at the same time they will accept without any question the belief that each one of us will be judged when we leave this earth according to his or her deeds during our lives here in mortality. Isn't it just as reasonable to believe that what we have received here in this earth life was given to each of us according to the merits of our conduct before we came here?" ("Understanding Who We Are Brings Self-Respect," *Ensign,* January 1974, 5).

For What Purpose Were You Chosen?

President Gordon B. Hinckley said this: "You are good. But it is not enough just to be good. You must be good for something. You must contribute good to the world. The world must be a better place for your presence. And the good that is in you must be spread to others. . . .

"But in this world so filled with problems, so constantly threatened by dark and evil challenges, you can and must rise above mediocrity, above indifference. You can become involved and speak with a strong voice for that which is right" ("Stand Up for Truth," in

Brigham Young University 1996–97 Speeches [Provo: Brigham Young University Press, 1997], 22).

President Spencer W. Kimball taught that before we were born we made sacred covenants with our Heavenly Father that, if we were allowed to be part of the youth of the noble birthright, we would stand for that which is right and make a difference in the world in which we live. He explained: "We have made covenants. We made them before we accepted our position here on the earth. . . .

" . . . We committed ourselves to our Heavenly Father. . . . This was a solemn oath, a solemn promise" (*Be Ye Therefore Perfect* [Salt Lake Institute of Religion Devotional, January 10, 1975], 2).

With your great premortal legacy comes the greatest responsibility ever placed upon a group of people in the history of the world. Read the following excerpts from President Hinckley regarding your noble and great generation:

"[You're] not just here by chance. You are here under the design of God" (*Teachings of Gordon B. Hinckley,* 720).

"Truly, my dear young friends, you are a chosen generation. I hope you will never forget it. I hope you will never take it for granted" ("'A Chosen Generation,'" *Ensign,* May 1992, 70).

"Never forget that you were chosen and brought to earth as a child of God for something of importance in his grand design. He expects marvelous things of you!" ("News of the Church," *Ensign,* February 1983, 76).

"We are on stage, you and I, at this glorious season. We have so much to do, so very, very much to *do to move forward the work of the Lord toward the marvelous destiny which He has outlined for it.* . . . None has a more compelling responsibility than do you. You are young. You have energy. You have convictions in your hearts. . . . I challenge you to stand for that which is right and true and good. . . . Regardless of your way of doing things in the past, I offer you a challenge to square your lives with the teachings of the gospel, . . . to live your life as an example of what the gospel of Jesus Christ will do in bringing happiness to an individual" ("True to the Faith," Salt Lake Valley-Wide Institute Fireside, January 21, 1996).

Another prophet of God, President Spencer W. Kimball, said this: "If the . . . members of the Church would live the gospel principles all the errors of the world would evaporate. The world would come to us, and we would change the frustration of the world to the peace of the gospel" (in "President Kimball Enjoys His Work," *Church News,* 26 February 1972, 13).

How Can You Keep the Promises You Made before You Were Born?

I have met young people all over the Church who have lived up to their premortal promises and are truly "youth of the noble birthright" in name and in deed. They are changing their world by standing up for that which is right and true and good, "at all times and in all things, and in all places" (Mosiah 18:9).

One such young man was Rick, an all-state running back on his high school football team. One day I was working in my office when he came in to see me.

"I need some help, Brother Bartholomew," he started.

"Okay, what can I do for you?"

"Well . . . there is a swearing problem with many of the LDS guys on the team, especially the seniors. Some of the younger guys are starting to swear just to impress them."

I knew many of these young men, and I was a little surprised to hear that. "Oh . . ." I replied, "So . . ."

"I've decided to ask each one of them, starting with the team captains, to stop swearing at the practices and games and start setting a better example for the younger players. . . . But those guys are *tough,* Brother Bartholomew . . . I'm afraid of what might happen if I start preaching to them . . ."

They *were* an unusually tough group of young men. But Rick

was a star athlete, and I knew he had the respect of the entire team. If anyone could get through to them, it was probably him.

"I think you'll be okay. Why don't you talk to a couple of them and see what happens?" I replied, trying to be encouraging.

Still unsure, but totally committed, Rick left my office.

Several weeks passed, and I had completely forgotten about our conversation in my office. Then one day in class when we were discussing the Aaronic Priesthood, I posed this question: "Does anyone know someone who is a good example of an Aaronic Priesthood holder?" To my surprise, several young men on the football team raised their hands all at once! As they all looked at each other and realized what had just happened, they were shocked. They were good guys, but they had never responded to any question I had ever asked with that kind of enthusiasm!

I pointed to one of them, who immediately blurted out, "Rick!"

"Why?" I asked.

In a serious tone, he recounted how Rick had approached him one day after practice and had asked him to start setting a better example for the other guys on the team by not swearing. He said Rick had done it in such a way as not to offend him, and that it had actually motivated him to clean up his language.

No sooner had the young man shared his experience than the other football players began to share similar experiences. Each of these young men realized that Rick had taken the time to talk to them individually about this difficult and personal issue.

I wish you could have seen the looks on their faces as these young men became aware that one of their friends had cared enough about them, the gospel, and the other LDS young men on the team to take a stand. Rick changed the world he lived in that year because he wasn't afraid to stand up for what was right and good and true.

Heather is another young person who wasn't afraid to take a stand in a difficult situation. Though she is a beautiful girl, she didn't date as much as she would have liked to during high school. After class one day she burst into my office: "*He* asked me out, Brother Bartholomew!"

"Who?" I asked.

"*He* did," came her reply. "It's one thing to get a date," she explained, "but I've been waiting for *this guy* to ask me out, and he did!"

When the day of their date finally arrived, I asked her: "Where is prince charming taking you tonight?"

"To the movie. I hope it is a good one."

"Well, he is a nice guy, isn't he?" I asked.

"He is a *great* guy," she responded, and with that she was off to class.

The next day I could hardly wait to ask her about her date. "So, how was it?"

"It was wonderful," she replied, "but it sure got off to a scary start! As we were walking across the parking lot toward the theater, I scanned the movie titles and ratings and realized there was only one good movie, and it was rated G!"

Heather had set a pretty high standard for herself. She had listened carefully to *everything* the prophets and apostles had said. She knew they had specifically asked us not to view R-rated movies, but she also knew they had also asked us not to view anything that is "vulgar, immoral, inappropriate, suggestive, or pornographic in any way" (*For the Strength of Youth* [Salt Lake City: The Church of Jesus Christ of Latter-day Saints, 1990], 12). She had told me that if the movie industry didn't think her little brothers and sisters should be seeing a particular movie because of violent or inappropriate content, it would probably be offensive to the Spirit as well. So, she had set a personal standard not to view any PG-13 movie or even some PG movies if they were questionable in any way. Her personal motto was this: "Keeping the companionship of the Holy Ghost is more important than a movie—*any* movie."

As they approached the ticket booth, she heard the young man ask for two tickets to a very popular movie. Her heart sunk. What was she going to do? She had wanted to make a good impression on her first date with him, but she knew this particular movie was inappropriate by any gospel standard. Everyone at school who had seen it had raved about it, but she knew from their description of it that it contained several scenes that would be completely offensive to the Holy Ghost. As she stood there, a line from the Young Women theme popped into her mind: "[I] will stand as a witness of God at all times and in all things, and in all places as [I] strive to live . . ." Nervously, she leaned over and whispered to her date: "I'm sorry, but I don't watch those kind of movies."

Startled, his face went from shock to relief as he blurted out, "Really? Neither do I!" He apologetically explained how he had truly wanted to impress her and had decided, against his own best judgment, to take her to this movie because of its popularity among their peers. They laughed out loud, bought two tickets to *Anastasia,* and enjoyed the rest of the evening together.

Heather is on a mission in Argentina at the time of this writing. As I have watched her over the years, I have noticed the profound effect she has had on many people. She has truly stood as a witness of God "at all times and in all things, and in all places."

Standing as a witness is doing what Jesus would do if he were here. It doesn't always mean that you'll have to defend the standards of the Church; sometimes it just calls for treating others the way the Savior would—even when it is inconvenient. I saw a remarkable example of this in a young woman named Kristen. She served as a student leader at the school where I taught seminary. She changed her world by treating others in a Christlike manner.

Because of her position, she spent her fair share of time "up in front," conducting assemblies, planning student activities, and being a leader. She was in a position where she could really have an influence on her peers. But sometimes the *real* opportunities to do this came in unexpected ways.

One day while she was eating lunch with her friends, a group of special-needs students came by and sat down beside them. These special young people were physically and socially awkward. One of them was learning disabled to the point that she had to live in a care center close enough to the high school that she could attend the resource classes during the day. Her name was Robyn. She was the only African-American student in the entire school. These new friends were warmly welcomed into the group, and eating lunch together became a daily occurrence.

As the school year progressed, Kristen began to develop a love for Robyn. She would visit her at the care center and would often take her to sporting events and other student activities. Although this was not always easy or convenient, she freely gave the love the Savior would have given to this special daughter of our Heavenly Father.

One day, while Kristen was conducting a student assembly, Robyn saw her and unexpectedly stood up and began pushing her way towards the front of the room. All eyes watched as she worked her way up the aisle. When she reached Kristen, she threw her arms around her, pinning the microphone between them. This allowed everyone in the audience to hear her tender, heartfelt words over the loud speaker: "Kristen, I love you! You are the only friend I have!"

Robyn's sincere expression of love penetrated deep into Kristen's heart. Unable to control her emotions (or finish conducting the assembly), she ran off the stage, went home, and spent the rest of the day crying. How could someone so sweet, so full of love, and so innocent think that only one person in the whole world loved her?

Shortly after graduation, Robyn lost her life in a tragic automobile accident. However, she died knowing that someone loved her. Young people, you have an opportunity to make a difference. Seize the day! Kristen was able to make the world she lived in a better place because she treated people the way the Savior would—while she still had the chance.

Sometimes the Lord gives us a second chance to make a difference. If we fail to "stand as a witness" the first time, we shouldn't give up! I saw an example of this in a sweet young sister in Detroit, Michigan, named Mary. As one of the only members of the Church in her school, she knew she had a great responsibility to keep the commandments and show others the way to live. However, sometimes that is difficult when other things get in the way.

Mary had always been a great example to her friends at school and was willing to talk openly about the Church. Bobby, who was one of these friends, had actually developed an interest in the Church because of her. However, when he asked her to the end-of-the-year school dance, she decided to go even though it was several months before her sixteenth birthday. *After all,* she thought, *it is just a big group of friends.* When an article appeared in the *New Era* a short time later about the dating standards of the Church, she read it and realized she had made a mistake.

She invited Bobby over one day and read the entire article to him. Confused, he asked her if they were breaking up before they had really even gotten together. Mary explained her feelings about these standards to him, and he agreed to just hang out as friends until her sixteenth birthday. In the meantime, she invited him to attend Mutual, sacrament meeting, and even an occasional family home evening .

When Mary turned sixteen, she began to date other young men as well as Bobby. Jealous and angry, he broke off their relationship and began spreading untrue things about Mary and the Church. Mary's mother tried to comfort her but finally decided to take matters into her own hands. She went to talk to Bobby herself and explained that if he was really that interested in Mary, he should take the time to find out what she was all about. He did. At Mary's invitation, he began to take the missionary discussions.

Shortly after that, Bobby's father unexpectedly passed away. Because of what the missionaries had taught him, he knew where his father was and how they could be together forever as a family again someday. He and his father had been very close, and this newfound knowledge of the gospel gave him the strength to endure the most difficult trial of his life to that point.

I met Bobby at their stake youth conference. As the chairman of the stake youth committee, he conducted the meetings. I was so impressed with him, and also with Mary. Several months later, I called to see how he was doing. He had been a star on the football team his junior year and was being actively recruited by several colleges. I asked him how his senior year was going and which college he had decided to sign with. His response took me by surprise. He said: "I'm not playing football this year, Brother Bartholomew. My mother was having a hard time making ends meet since my father's death, and so I decided to take on a part-time job to help out with the family finances. Besides, I have to start saving for my mission, right?"

Look at the difference that was made in one man's life because a young woman was willing to take a stand. Even though she made a mistake along the way, she went back and made it right. As a result a young man in her world found the Savior and his gospel, was able to make it through the loss of his father, and serve faithfully in the Church.

My young friends, remember who you are. Remember that you made promises to our Father in Heaven who sent you here to this earth "for such a time as this" (Esther 4:14). As the "youth of the noble birthright" you can and will make a difference as you "stand as witnesses of God at all times and in all things, and in all places" (Mosiah 18:9).

Ron Bartholomew served a full-time mission in Pusan, Korea. He received bachelor's and master's degrees from Brigham Young University. He married Kristen Buckwalter, and they are the parents of seven children. For the past eighteen years he has taught released-time seminary in Utah and Idaho. He is currently teaching part-time in the Department of Ancient Scripture at BYU and full-time at the LDS Institute of Religion adjacent to Utah Valley State College. He is currently serving as a Sunday School teacher in his ward. He enjoys walks with his wife, doing homework with his children, and gardening.

17

FINDING THE LIGHT OF THE LORD IN DEEP WATERS AND DARK TIMES

A. David Thomas

I am afraid of snakes, and I have been afraid of the dark. I've felt fear, even terror, at the thought of speaking in front of people and being judged or evaluated by others. I've been a worrier all my life, and I have a vivid imagination. I've spent more than my fair share of time in the dark and in deep water. I think I'm an expert on fear.

When the Lord, through the scriptures, speaks about fear, he identifies two kinds. The first is desirable. This kind of fear is called a "fear of the Lord" (Mosiah 4:1). This fear implies a reverence, an awe, and a deep respect for God, his ways, commandments, and plan, and suggests that we should back away from anything that could risk, frustrate, or in any way imperil our ability to be with and on God's side. This fear is productive and proactive. This fear is sensible and justified. Paul called this fear "godly fear" (Hebrews 12:28).

A second kind of fear that is identified in the scriptures seems to stupefy and stall righteous action. The Lord and his prophets would have us avoid this destructive fear. Unproductive fear can be cast out with love (see Moroni 8:16), righteousness (see D&C 6:33-34), and preparation (see D&C 38:30). Our Heavenly Father would have us push through fears that cause doubts and hesitations because they remove the blessings that come from faith-filled action: "Ye endeavored to believe that ye should receive the blessing which was offered unto you; but . . . there were fears in your hearts, and . . . this is the reason that ye did not receive" (D&C 67:3).

But a careful reading of the scriptures reveals that, with the possible exception of Jesus, many if not all of the "noble and great ones" have at some time suffered from unproductive fear. Gideon needed some sheepskin miracles to overcome his fears and become the Lord's "mighty man of valour" (Judges 6:12; see vv. 36–40). Jacob's fear of the revenge of his brother, Esau, caused him to take elaborate precautions and seek to placate Esau with gifts (see Genesis 32:6–20). Even the young Joseph Smith "was ready to sink into despair and abandon [himself] to destruction" (Joseph Smith— History 1:16). It would appear that there is an interaction or conflict between righteous and unproductive fears, and that this conflict is the appropriate lot of those who have come to earth to fulfill our Heavenly Father's plan.

The prophet Moses provides a good example of the interaction of the two fears. The Old Testament tells us that Moses was the meekest of men (see Numbers 12:3). We think of meek as meaning being teachable, submissive, and patient—all worthy attributes. But the Moses we meet in Exodus chapter 4 sounds afraid of the assignment. Moses began to make excuses to the Lord, suggesting reasons why he was the wrong man for the job.

The Lord called him to be His spokesman, and Moses replied, "They will not believe me, nor hearken unto my voice" (Exodus 4:1). But the Lord assured him that they would, and He provided Moses with some signs or miracles to convince the unbelievers. The Lord taught him how to turn his staff into a snake and back into a staff. He also provided a leprous-hand miracle that I'm sure impressed Moses, because it was Moses' hand that the Lord turned white with the disease and then healed. Then the Lord showed

Moses how to change water into blood. But in spite of the Lord's effort to persuade, Moses held his ground. He said, "I am not eloquent . . . but I am slow of speech, and of a slow tongue."

The Lord tried again. He said, "I will be with thy mouth, and teach thee what thou shalt say." But Moses pleaded with the Lord to send someone else. The scriptures indicate that the Lord now was angry with Moses because of his fears. He gave Moses his brother, Aaron, as a spokesman. The Lord said, "He shall be to thee instead of a mouth, and thou shalt be to him instead of God. . . . and [I] will teach you what ye shall do." (Exodus 4:1, 10, 12, 15, 16.)

The important lesson here is that in spite of his fears, Moses went. He mastered those fears and threw his staff in at Pharaoh's feet, where as a serpent it swallowed the magicians' rod (serpents) while Aaron spoke boldly the words of God that came from Moses' lips. Ten times Moses fought for God against the power of Egypt and its pharaoh, until the most arrogant of men bowed his will to the words of the meekest of men and the children of Israel were set free.

Prophets or ordinary sinners, we all have our fears. As I've told you, I have been afraid of the dark. I was the victim of a wonderful imagination. To my unenlightened mind the absence of light meant the presence of horrible things. I would quiver in the sheets of my bed and assume the walls were covered with spiders; the floor crawled with snakes and ghouls; and the air vibrated with demons, banshees, and ghosts, just waiting for me to let my guard down. Now, this was not the problem of a small child but rather a young man well on his way into high school, and my father, a sensitive man, realized I was distressed, because fifteen-year-olds normally don't want to sleep with their parents.

"What is it, son?" he asked from his bed.

"Nothing," I replied, but my eyes were wide with fear, and my body was covered with sweat.

My dad pulled back the sheets and got up. He walked me into

the living room. We sat down. "You're frightened, aren't you?" he said.

"Yes!"

"Of what?"

"I don't know."

These are the times when good fathers pass muster. "You know, son," my father started, "when I was your age, living in Varteg, Wales, I had to walk down the hill and get water out of a well for my mother. It seemed to me that your grandmother always wanted water in the middle of the night. I always tried to talk her out of it, but mothers don't always listen to fifteen-year-old boys, and I would find myself out in the dark, afraid. In my mind, son, the night was filled with frightful things. In my mind, the worst of things lived in the dark. Somehow your grandfather sensed my fears, and one night he walked into the dark with me." (I don't know why, but my father and I were sitting in the dark. We hadn't turned on the lights.)

"My dad, your grandpa, told me to look up at the sky, and we looked at it together. He told me of pictures in the sky, framed with stars. He reminded me of warm summer breezes and moonlight. We talked of winter nights, and stars dropping their light, and the new snow sparkling back the favor. He talked of the future, girls, love, and again of moonlight. He told me of rest, sleep, and beautiful dreams, all products of the nighttime. And he reminded me that a child, the Light of the world, came down to us in the dark, at night-time. Your grandfather explained that fear of the dark or other things is the first test of growing up. To be full tall we must face our fears, push through, and see the beauty on the other side."

My dad and I walked outside. We looked at the stars, and then we both went to bed and slept well.

So much of unproductive fear is a matter of how you see it. My dad, as his dad had done, simply expanded my definition of the dark; and with a new view, with time, and with the moonlight, my fear of the dark went away.

Life is full of these kinds of transitional fears, fears we have to face, interpret, and move through. All of us have to intersect and pass through our fears. Nephi had to resist his fear of change and allow the Lord to soften his heart so that he didn't rebel, as his older brothers did (see 1 Nephi 2:16). Adam and Eve accepted death in order that we might exist in mortality (see Moses 5:11). Esther risked her station as queen and also her life to plead for the lives of her people (see Esther 4:11, 14; 5:1–2). Noah, Lehi, the brother of Jared, and Joseph Smith each risked humiliation to warn a people and save their children. Hannah took risks and covenanted with the Lord for a son; and when the Lord blessed her with one, she kept her promise and returned him to God, thus giving Israel the prophet Samuel (see 1 Samuel 1–3). And Abraham, living in a wicked world, looked past its ugliness and courageously sought the blessings of the fathers (see Abraham 1:1–4). Fear is always there just trying to get a hold on us. It can be both our nemesis and our friend. Fear can keep us from becoming ourselves, but it can also keep us from danger. How can we know the difference between righteous and non-productive fear?

A friend of mine, Dr. Lynn Johnson, told me a disturbing story. It seems that in the northern parts of Wisconsin the lake water never really gets warm. The ice barely melts from the surface of the lakes before the winter snow begins to fall. As a result, lake swimming is not big in those northern parts of Wisconsin, and in remote areas where there are no heated, covered pools, many people never learn to swim.

One day in late summer, in one of these cold water areas, a group of teenagers was having a party on the edge of a lake. Part of the group was playing on a boat dock that reached far out into the lake, and as a result of a playful struggle, one of the boys was knocked into the water. He screamed out in terror that he could not swim, and he fought frantically to keep from sinking. The other young people struggled to reach him, but he was beyond their reach, and there wasn't a swimmer among them. The boy thrashed desperately to reach for them as they in turn groped hopelessly for him. Finally, realizing their dilemma, two boys ran to get the park ranger. Running both ways, they quickly returned with the ranger, but to their heartache they found their friend floating face down in the water.

It was then that something truly shocking happened. The ranger waded out into the water right up to the side of the corpse of the drowned boy. It was only waist deep. If the boy had only stood up, he could have walked out of the lake, but in his fear he died, helpless in a totally manageable situation.

The Lord would have us master our fears of just trying life out. We must all learn to swim in the struggles of just being alive and becoming ourselves. Doing is living. We mustn't be afraid of "having a go." Fear that keeps us from becoming and obeying is unproductive fear.

Florence Chadwick of California was a remarkable swimmer. She was the first woman to swim the English Channel from England to France, which she did in sixteen hours and nineteen minutes on 11 September 1953. Later she would swim that channel two other times. The total point-to-point distance was twenty-one miles, but allowing for crosscurrents, experts placed the actual swimming distance at closer to fifty miles.

Florence was truly a remarkable swimmer, and that's what makes what happened on 4 July 1952 so strange. The swim was to Catalina Island, twenty-one miles off the coast of southern California. She started her swim using the deep hard strokes she had developed swimming off the coast of San Diego. The swim continued without a hitch until she was just a half mile from the Catalina coast, at which point she raised up in the water to see how much further she had to go. The coast was shrouded in fog; she could not see her goal; and to the amazement of those rowing in her support boat, she quit and climbed into the boat. Her support crew could hear the surf crashing against the Catalina coast, but Florence saw only fog; she couldn't see the coast, so she quit.

The devil loves this kind of fear-induced failure because the hero has already paid the price of conquest, but he or she leaves the field empty-handed and dejected. Discouragement is an ugly form of fear, and in a righteous cause, it can be overcome with the aid of prayer, scripture study, service, and the support of friends.

While discouragement and doubt are ugly forms of unproductive fear, not all fear is bad. Some fear comes as a warning—a warning to back away, to quit. These fears warn that the risk is too high and not worth the cost. This is a fear we all need to recognize and heed. Such fears alert us that we are entering evil and forbidden waters.

On 25 August 1875, Captain Matthew Webb became the first human to swim the English Channel unassisted. This swim would make him famous; the press would acknowledge him as the world's greatest swimmer. Thousands flocked to see him swim using the stroke that conquered the channel. He gave demonstrations of his endurance. At one point he won four hundred English pounds for swimming more than seventy-four hours. Progressively, he became more of a stuntman than an athlete, hence he yearned for another great swim. As his popularity waned in England, he moved to the United States, where he and his manager continued to look for the "Big One." Captain Webb needed to make some real money. He had a wife and two children to support.

And then they found it—the elusive "Big One!" It was Niagara Falls. Below those falls lay a stretch of the angriest water on the face of the earth. If Webb could swim it, his fame would be restored.

On a late summer day in 1883, the thirty-five-year-old, two-hundred-pound swimmer stood on the edge of the Niagara River just below the falls. At this point the river funnels into two steep walls, causing the speed of the water to accelerate to over thirty-five miles per hour. The surface of the water billows with angry waves, some reaching over twenty-five feet high. Then the river cascades into the whirlpool rapids, which continue for over a mile, and below these rapids the whirlpool itself gapes hungry for the stupid. Webb saw all of this. His only comment was, "It's a rum bit of water."

In spite of wiser counsel, he got into a boat and was rowed out into the center of the river, where he jumped in and started swimming. Five hundred spectators watched this foolhardy enterprise. With powerful strokes Webb pulled toward the whirlpool rapids. Then he disappeared. The water just swallowed him. The swim lasted only four minutes, and the body was not found for four days. He had been caught by those furious waters, and he died in mid-stroke. The doctors who examined the body said that the force of the water had pressed the life right out of him. For a past-the-prime effort to recapture the "Big One," he left his wife and two children with no support. A wise sense of fear said "back off," but he didn't listen.

So some fears must be worked through, and others offer a whispered "back away." How we interact with these fears determines the quality and scope of our life.

A proper response to a fear can leave us with a magnificent memory. A few years back, I had a goal, a dream. I was going to Egypt, and I wanted to run in the morning desert sun from the Sphinx to the Pyramids of Giza. A short run, but it would be a memorable one. I held a vision in my heart and mind of me racing across the deserts of Cairo as the sun danced on the eternal steps of Cheops.

I arrived in Egypt at the height of Ramadan, a month-long period of fasting that all devout Muslims observe. From dawn to darkness each day of that month, the faithful of Islam fast to purify their lives and thereby produce extra food and money for the poor. Cairo is unbelievable at Ramadan, especially at night. Colored lights hang everywhere, and the faithful fill the streets as at dark they rush to happily end their daily fast. As I watched that first night, the eager hungry pressed against each other and the side of the bus. The noise and the strangeness of this new world frightened me, and I was glad I sat safely with people I knew. My first night in Africa was a frightening one, especially for someone who had a history of being afraid—afraid of the dark and of the unknown.

Well, my days in Egypt passed quickly, and soon my last day turned from daylight to dark. I had not fulfilled my desert dream run. Outside, after days of my learning to understand and appreciate Muslim ways and Muslim people, the noise and dark of Ramadan waited along with the Sphinx and the pyramids. I ran out into the dark. I ran past the happy Egyptians eating and rejoicing in their faith. I ran up to the ancient face of the Sphinx and said my good-byes, and then I turned and ran up the hill to the majesty of the Pyramids of Giza. Thus, with the lights of Cairo flickering behind me, I fulfilled a daylight dream in the dark I had once feared.

I pray that you will overcome your foolish fears and be responsive to all of your righteous ones.

David Thomas is an instructor at the Salt Lake Institute of Religion at the University of Utah and an instructor of business at the University of Phoenix in Salt Lake City. Holding a doctorate in education, Brother Thomas has taught in youth and family programs at Brigham Young University. He is the author of There Are No Dragons Out There. *Besides writing, his interests include reading, running, swimming, and traveling. He and his wife, Paula, have six children and ten grandchildren.*

18

REAL LOVE—THE MOST AWESOME ADVENTURE

Suzanne L. Hansen

I heard of a young man who had such a great need to be loved by a particular young lady that he sent her a special delivery letter every day for sixty days. On the sixty-first day, she announced she was in love with the mailman and that they would marry.

All joking aside, let's face it. Most of us have a strong, overwhelming need to be loved. Love is needed in order to survive, and we need it from our earliest beginnings. Countless studies have shown that human babies need to be held, cuddled, and spoken to lovingly, from the moment of birth. When they are loved, people grow and mature into healthy adults. Without it, they may sicken both physically and emotionally, and may even die. Love is as important to our health and well-being as good food.

In my experience with young people, I have discovered that many feel like Bennett Cerf in the following story.

Some years ago, a number of famous men and women were on a TV talk show discussing the things that made them most afraid. They agreed that they were afraid of powerful weapons that could annihilate the world. They also feared energy shortages, crime in the cities, and world pollution.

During most of the discussion, one man remained silent. Bennett Cerf, a journalist and TV commentator, was usually a very talkative man. That day, he sat very quietly, contributing nothing. Just as the show was about to end, the host said, "Well, Mr. Cerf, you haven't said much. Isn't there anything you really fear?"

In a quiet voice, Bennett Cerf answered, "There's only one thing I really fear—and that's not being loved."

We all crave love, just like plants crave water. And we do all sorts of funny, ridiculous, crazy, noble, special things to earn the love of other people. We also sing, dance, write, play an instrument, or participate in some kind of sport—and we do it partly for the approval of others and the applause of the crowd.

Basically, there are takers and there are givers of love. Takers fear they won't have love. Albert Einstein once said, "We're either full of love, or full of fear."

Takers seem to demand love and tend to draw it from others, without offering any in return. Have you ever been around anyone like that? You might hear a taker say, "Why haven't you called me lately? I've been waiting to hear from you." These people want the loving feeling that comes from knowing that another friend wants to talk to them, but they do not see the need to call that friend.

Have you been around people who "hog" a conversation with repeated stories about *their* school, friends, people at work, clothes, and dates? Very quickly we are boxed out of the conversation while our friend is intoxicated with himself or herself, glancing up only to make sure that someone is still listening.

Such people often have low self-esteem, and they seek the admiration and attention of others in order to feel worthwhile. Ultimately, they push so hard for this attention and acceptance that no one can stand to be their friend. It seems strange, doesn't it, when all along all they wanted was to be loved.

Some people learn to rely upon the feelings they derive from using drugs, alcohol, and premarital sex as substitutes for real love. All of these provide a false sense of well-being, but the effects are only temporary and not truly fulfilling.

Then there are the benefits that come to the givers of love. I've found that the one sure way of getting love is to give it. It's been said that life gives to the giver and takes from the taker. I believe that a lost opportunity to give love is a lost opportunity to receive love.

The story is told about a young man who was having a difficult time. He decided to take a break from his troubles and visit someone who needed a lift. He walked into a convalescent home, made his way to the desk, and asked if he might see anyone who could use a visit. He approached those people and said with a smile, "Hello, I'm the official hugger around here. I've just come to share a bit of sunshine. I'd like to give you a hug."

The older people loved getting a hug. This sincere young man made them feel loved, vital, and alive. And in return, he felt worthwhile and loved. As he was leaving, many reached out and grabbed and kissed his hand as tears streamed down their cheeks. As he drove home, his burdens seemed lighter.

Even though we all want to be loved, we sometimes forget the simple things we can do to *give* love. These steps will bring more abundant love into your life as you give love.

Step 1—Speak Loving Words

When we're kind and tender in the way we talk with others, whether they are strangers or closely related to us, we are offering them love.

Unfortunately, people often abuse each other with harsh words. Remember, we are known to others, perhaps more than anything else, *by the words we speak.* Having a positive, loving attitude when speaking to anyone can brighten some of the darkest days.

Al Sizer lives in Portland, Oregon. He decided to go out to eat at an excellent restaurant called Daiseys. When Al arrived, the line for a table was already a half-block long, so he agreed to sit at the counter. Sitting next to him was a downcast, withdrawn man who apparently didn't want to be disturbed.

But Al has a wonderful, effervescent, positive personality, and he began talking to the man and finally broke through his shell. They talked together for almost two hours. Then Al realized he had an appointment, gave his business card to the man, and left, never expecting to hear from him again.

The next week the man from the restaurant came to Al's office with tears in his eyes, saying, "Al, you saved my life."

Al was flabbergasted. The man poured out his story. Just hours before they had met at Daiseys, a doctor had told this man that his X rays showed he had a terminal illness, one that would prove to be very painful toward the end. On the spot, the fellow had decided to commit suicide, rather than have to experience such a horrible death. But he decided to first have one last meal at his favorite restaurant. And that's how he came to be at Daiseys, where he met Al.

Al had spoken to him so kindly and affirmatively about families and caring that he had decided not to end his life that day, and not to deprive his wife and children of the few months that might be left to him.

A week later, he had gone back to the doctor and had learned that his X rays had somehow been switched or mixed-up with someone else's. He didn't actually have the illness he had feared. If he had not had that conversation with Al, he would have needlessly ended his life.

We never know what effect a soft, kind word will have on another person, or how important a listening ear will be to someone else. Just caring enough to give the "I care" message may be all that is needed to even save a life.

Step 2—Writing Love Notes

A love note is an excellent way to communicate love to another person. When the person receives it, he or she will feel warm and loved. And you will feel better for having written it.

Notes can be hidden to be found in purses, pockets, lockers, cupboards, pillows, or in other fun, unexpected places. Several weeks after my uncle died, his wife found a love note he had written to her and hidden in a place where she would find it when she was cleaning. It touched her deeply and helped her feel close to him in her time of loss.

Love notes are vitally important, especially to grandparents, friends, or loved ones who, just like you, need a lift. Teachers and others who serve us also need to know how much we appreciate them.

As a man lay on his deathbed, his wife said, "Dear, all these years we have lived together and not once have you ever told me that you loved me—not a note, not a flower, not even a word. Am I not worthy of your love?"

He explained, "I told you I loved you on the day we got married, and I didn't think I needed to repeat myself."

No one can hear too many loving thoughts or enough kind words.

Step 3—Give a Hug

A national hug survey was reported by Mark Victor Hansen, author of *Dare to Win.* In that survey, it was discovered that 83 percent of the people surveyed grew up getting less than a hug a day. Even if we are reluctant to admit it out loud, 99 percent of us want more hugs.

Dr. Dean McGraine, a psychologist, suggested that everyone needs a minimum of four hugs a day. The requirement for maximum emotional growth is twelve hugs a day. If your family members initially resist your hugs, just explain to them you're involved in a special high-tech hugging experiment—that you would like them to be the co-hugger with you for twelve hugs a day. Explain that hugging has positive effects on people. It has been shown to increase the rate of language development, IQ, and self-esteem.

Remember, you aren't making a sexual statement by giving a hug. You're making a statement about human love and caring. In the language of my Scandinavian forefathers, the Norse word *hugga* means "to comfort, hold close, or to console."

Sometimes it's wise to ask permission to give a hug. Some

people have a hard time accepting them. Even though they really need them, they may not be accustomed to either receiving or giving them. But they'll love it.

Step 4—Act with Love

Actions speak louder than any words. If you care about people, how do you show your love?

On a rainy day in New York, around the turn of the century, a disheveled, older lady stepped into a department store to get out of the weather. She asked several people for help.

Because she was dripping wet and appeared to be penniless, no one wanted to bother with her. Everyone seemed to be irritated by her, except for one young salesman who said, "Would you like a chair while you wait for someone to come and pick you up?" And then he arranged for a taxi for her.

Before she left, she said, "Young man, please write down your name and address on a piece of paper and give it to me." And he did so. The next day, Andrew Carnegie, this lady's son and one of the richest men in the world at that time, called the store. He said that he wanted to buy enough furniture to fill a Scottish castle he had just purchased. And he said that he wanted to make certain the commission on the sale went to the young man who had treated his mother so kindly. Furthermore, he was inviting the young man to accompany the family to Scotland to help arrange the furnishings in the castle.

The manager of the store protested and said he was fearful the young salesman didn't have enough experience to handle such an assignment. Mr. Carnegie disagreed, saying, "My mother said the young man treated her with great care and kindness, even though he didn't know who she was. With that kind of concern, he'll care enough to do the job correctly."

Step 5—Smile

A smile—a simple smile—is like the warmth of the sun. It has the power to brighten a person's entire day—sometimes an entire life. It sends a message of your love and is a mirror to your soul. So smile often: In elevators. At people in cars. In stores. At classmates. At sales clerks. And, especially, at your family members.

More often than not, your smile will be returned, and not only will you have made someone else's day just a bit brighter, yours will be brighter as well.

People who are busy loving others don't have much time to brood on whether others love them or not. Remember, love is available in abundance, if we give our love away.

An example of this great truth is found in the book *Dare to Win,* by Mark Victor Hansen. Linda Birtish, an accomplished artist and poet, died at the young age of twenty-eight of a brain tumor. She had never married but had drawn a picture in her last days of what she imagined her ideal man would have looked like. Perhaps some of you will recall seeing this story on the television show *20/20.*

In a final act of love, she arranged to give herself away. She donated all the useful parts of her body to be used in transplants. Her eyes went to an eye bank in Bethesda, Maryland, and from there to a recipient in South Carolina. A twenty-eight-year-old man was given the gift of sight by Linda's gift of love.

He was profoundly grateful and wrote to the eye bank to thank them for the good work they do. (Incidentally, this "love note" was only the second thank-you note they had received from a recipient of any of the over 30,000 eyes they had processed.)

But this grateful fellow wanted to go even further. He wanted to thank Linda's parents for her and for her generous act of love and service. There was an immediate bond of love established between the young man and Linda's folks, and they invited him to stay in their home for the weekend.

He slept in Linda's room, where he noticed that some of her favorite books were the ones he had learned to enjoy in braille. The next morning, Linda's mother made the comment that he looked familiar. She was sure she had seen him somewhere before.

Remembering, Linda's mother then ran upstairs and pulled out the last picture that her artist-daughter had ever drawn. It was a picture of her ideal man, and the likeness was virtually identical to the man who had received her eyes. Then her mother read him the last poem Linda had written, even on her deathbed. It read:

> *Two hearts passing in the night*
> *Falling in love*
> *Never able to gain each other's sight.*

One of the most beautiful scriptures about love was written by Moroni as he was closing the Book of Mormon. He wrote of the "pure love of Christ," which is at the root of all that is good in our world (see Moroni 7:47). Moroni saw what happened to his people because they didn't have this charity.

And for us, may we strive for this love every day. The Apostle Paul described it clearly. "Charity suffereth long, and is kind; charity envieth not; charity vaunteth not itself, is not puffed up, doth not behave itself unseemly, seeketh not her own, is not easily provoked, thinketh no evil; rejoiceth not in iniquity, but rejoiceth in the truth" (1 Corinthians 13:4–6).

Such love, Paul said, "never faileth" (v. 8). Now, that's *real* love!

Follow the five simple steps I've outlined, and you will feel love flooding into your life, as you give it to others. What an awesome adventure! You will have nothing to fear, and you will be numbered among the elect of God.

Suzanne Hansen was born in San Francisco, California, and is married to Michael D. Hansen. They are proud parents of three children: Jenny, John, and Julie. Suzanne is the author of five books and three tape programs. She was Honor Mother for the state of Utah in 1980 and has served in the Young Women organization for much of the last twenty years.

19

PORNOGRAPHY: SATAN'S COUNTERFEIT

Brad Wilcox

In 1996 the United States Treasury issued a new design of the hundred-dollar bill. I never saw it because Ben Franklin and I don't spend a lot of time together, but when the new fifties and twenties started showing up a few years later I got to examine some new currency. "It looks like play money," I told the bank teller. "I feel like we're starting a Monopoly game."

"It's real," she assured me.

"Why did they change it?" I asked.

She explained that in our high-tech society it was becoming much too easy to counterfeit the former bills. "These new notes have more security features built in," she said. "It's easier to spot the forgeries."

It's good they made the change. I wouldn't want to get stuck with any counterfeit bills. I once read of a man who spent several days helping to unload, clean, and reload a huge truck, only to be paid in counterfeit money. At first he didn't notice. In fact, he was excited because he thought the truck driver had been extremely generous. The man thanked the driver profusely as he left. Then the man tried to buy something at a store. The cashier took his money, looked at it, and called over the manager. The manager examined the bills and told the man his money was unacceptable.

Suddenly the guy wasn't feeling so grateful to that truck driver. In fact, he was furious. He couldn't believe the driver would intentionally deceive him. He was embarrassed in front of the cashier and store manager. He felt bitter, angry, and discouraged that he had nothing to show for his time and effort but a handful of worthless forgeries.

When I read that story, I felt sorry for the man but not nearly as sorry as I feel for young people who get stuck with a different kind of forgery. The man lost some money. Some young people I know are in danger of losing a lot more because they are accepting a counterfeit from Satan called pornography.

What is more beautiful than the human body? What is more wonderful and pure than true love between husband and wife? These sacred things have incredible eternal value. No wonder Satan tries to counterfeit them. Are we going to accept his cheap imitations? Are we going to let Satan rip us off?

Not many of us can spot a counterfeit bill. At first many do not recognize Satan's frauds either. Like the man who was excited to receive the truck driver's money, too many get excited about pornography only to find out later that what they assumed to be worthwhile is actually worthless.

One LDS young man I'll call Matt became involved with pornography when he was visiting at a friend's house and his friend showed him some magazine pictures. Matt says, "I had always heard pornography described as dirty, smutty, filthy, and ugly. But what I saw in those pictures didn't look all that ugly to me. It looked pretty appealing." Matt allowed himself to be fooled. He found himself tempted to view pornography more and more. He started to buy magazines, rent videos, and look up pornographic sites on the Internet. Matt says, "It wasn't hard to find once I started looking."

In the months that followed, Matt found himself less and less satisfied with the soft stuff. He says, "I wanted pictures that were more graphic and extreme." He soon found that his unworthy thoughts led to unworthy acts, one after another after another. Matt says, "I let my hormones override all my better judgment. Guilt, fear, and depression became my constant companions: guilt because I knew what I was doing was wrong; fear because I was terrified that my secret indulgences would be found out; and depression because I could no longer feel the Spirit. I began to hate myself."

Matt was caught in a dangerous downward cycle. In an effort to ease his depression, he would view pornography. Then he would become more depressed than before and once again turn to the pornography as a temporary escape. Matt explains, "I first started viewing pornography because it was exciting and gave me a rush. Later I no longer turned to pornography to feel good, but to stop from feeling bad." He was hooked. Just as surely as if he were heavily involved with drugs or alcohol, he was addicted.

Matt says, "Over and over I'd tell myself that I would never view pornography again. Then I'd go right ahead and do it." Like the man who received counterfeit bills from the truck driver, Matt realized that what he originally thought was something good was just a fake. Like the man, Matt felt embarrassed, bitter, and angry. He says, "I think of the time and money I spent on that stuff, and I feel sick. It affected my relationships with others, my Church activity, and my grades in school. It consumed my life, and I feel angry about that, but I know I have no one to blame but myself."

Empty-handed, brokenhearted, Matt finally found the courage to approach his bishop. With the help of his priesthood leader, he began the long process of repenting and breaking unworthy habits. Matt states, "Turning away from pornography has been the most difficult thing I have ever done. Sometimes it is such a battle to control my thoughts that by the end of the day I feel physically, emotionally, and spiritually drained. I would give anything if I had never started in the first place." I admire Matt's determination to repent and make positive changes. I appreciate him letting me share his story. He says, "Perhaps it can help others be smarter than I was. Maybe it can help them avoid my struggles."

How do we avoid getting sucked in? If some, like Matt, have been tempted in the past, how can unworthy habits be broken once and for all? The new money issued by the United States Treasury has security features. That's what we need too: ways to detect and reject Satan's counterfeit of pornography. On each new bill there is an enlarged portrait, a new background, microprinting, glowing thread, a number that shifts color when viewed from different angles, and a watermark that is visible when held to the light.

Enlarged Portrait

The enlarged portrait on the bills allows for more detail, which makes it harder to duplicate. As we seek for power to reject pornography, it helps to have an enlarged picture of ourselves, the details about who we are eternally and our role in Heavenly Father's plan.

Consider the significance of receiving, caring for, and honoring our bodies, bodies for which we longed during our premortal experience, bodies that Satan and his hosts will never have. No wonder they want us to disregard, disrespect, and abuse our own bodies and the bodies of others.

Consider the sacred nature of our procreative powers. Think of how the righteous use of these powers can bring us to God as he allows us to have families of our own. Within marriage, sexual relations are a wholesome tool that can be used to build incredible loving relationships between husbands and wives who are bonded together spiritually and emotionally as well as physically. No wonder Satan will do anything to degrade sex and tempt us to use that tool to destroy instead of build. Satan would have us use the very power that can bring us such unbelievable joy in unauthorized and selfish ways. He would have us settle for fleeting gratification over enduring happiness. We must keep an enlarged portrait of our eternal potential firmly in our minds. Then Satan's counterfeit can be seen for what it is.

New Background

Each new bill also has a new background behind the enlarged portrait. When trying to resist any temptation, it is helpful to modify our background, or environment. If I am trying to lose weight, I'd better not be hanging around the bakery. Similarly, those trying to quit drinking are foolish to enter bars. Those struggling with pornography must not allow themselves to go near certain stores or into the homes of certain friends. They would be wise to move their computers out of their bedrooms and into more public places, such as the living room or family room. If laptops present too great a temptation, it may be wise to get a parental protection program or an Internet filter and let someone else control the password.

The new backgrounds on the money are filled with lines. We must fill our new environments with lots of people and positive activities. When all else fails, in moments of temptation we need to follow the example of Joseph of old and simply run away (see Genesis 39:12). Then we will be more secure against Satan's counterfeit.

Microprinting

If you look closely at the new bills, you will see tiny words printed throughout the side borders and portraits. On the fifty-dollar bill, for example, take a good look at Grant's collar. Because the words are so small, microprinting is hard to duplicate and thus offers greater security. Isn't that the same in our lives? It's the little things that make the difference.

When my daughter was in second grade, we were having family night and I asked, "What can we do to be happy?" After a long pause, she exhaled loudly, rolled her eyes dramatically, and sighed, "Just . . . just do . . . all that stuff!"

At first I thought she was being silly, but the more I thought about it, the more I realized she was absolutely right. By "all that stuff," she meant to pray and read scriptures, Church-oriented books, and the *New Era* (and not just the joke page). We need to fast, bear our testimony, attend Church meetings, participate in Young Men and Young Women activities, and stay close to our parents and leaders. Sure, they are all small things, but "by small and simple things are great things brought to pass" (Alma 37:6).

Glowing Thread

The polymer thread that has been embedded vertically in the paper of the new bills glows yellow under ultraviolet light. This makes any counterfeit extremely easy to spot because it doesn't have a glowing thread. Similarly, a marriage that has been embedded with threads of trust, fidelity, and commitment glows with love. There is no love in pornography, only lust. There is no concern for another, only for self. There is no relationship to be strengthened, only nameless bodies, dehumanized sexual objects. Victor B. Cline stated that most pornography "presents highly inaccurate, unscientific, and distorted information about human sexuality. It is, in a sense, sex miseducation marketed for financial gain" (in *Encyclopedia of Mormonism,* Daniel H. Ludlow, ed., 5 vols. [New York: Macmillan Publishing Co., 1992], 3:1112). Where there is no love, there is no glow, and Satan's bill is seen for the dull, dark, and lifeless counterfeit it is.

Color Shifting

The numbers in the lower right corners of the new bills are printed in such a way that they appear green when viewed from straight on but black when viewed from an angle. It's called color shifting. Many in the world would try to convince us there are no absolutes when it comes to good or bad, that right and wrong exist only in our minds, and that what is moral or immoral depends completely on the angle from which it is viewed. Don't be fooled. The shifting colors on the new bills provide security, but the shifting values of the world do not. From any angle, pornography is wrong and sinful.

President Spencer W. Kimball stated, "Pornography pollutes the mind. The stench of obscenity and vulgarity reaches and offends the heavens. It putrifies all it touches. . . . Pornography and erotic stories and pictures are worse than polluted food. Shun them. The body has power to rid itself of sickening food. That person who entertains filthy stories or pornographic pictures and literature records them in his marvelous human computer, the brain, which can't forget this filth" (Edward L. Kimball, ed., *The Teachings of Spencer W. Kimball* [Salt Lake City: Bookcraft, 1982], 282–83).

I once attended a youth conference and stayed as a guest in the home of one of the adult leaders. This good brother and his wife made arrangements for their teenage son to stay over with friends so I could sleep in his room. As they led me upstairs, they apologized because their son, a priest, had chosen to cover the walls of his room with pictures of models and actresses wearing not much more than smiles. The father said, "I've talked to him, but he says I'm making a big deal out of nothing, that all his school friends do the same thing, and the pictures are really not that bad."

The words brought to mind some questions Elder Richard G. Scott of the Quorum of the Twelve Apostles asked during a talk at BYU: "Do you thirst after righteousness? Or are there times when the allure of stimulating images is allowed to temporarily fill your mind because, after all, they are really not that bad? Do your actions focus on entertainment, immediate satisfaction, self-interests, or personal gratification even though your goals are elsewhere?" ("Finding Happiness," in *1996–97 Speeches* [Provo, Utah: Brigham Young University Publications and Graphics, 1997], 360).

I left my bags in the room and went to the youth conference. Later that night when I returned to my host family's home and entered the young man's bedroom, I was immediately confronted by all the supposedly not-so-bad images and decided to take matters into my own hands. I found some paper and scissors and cut out a lot of circles like the ones you see coming from the mouths of cartoon characters in the comics. I then taped the paper bubbles next to the mouths of all the ladies and wrote comments like, "I'm going to marry only a returned missionary," "I want to be married in the temple," and "I am a daughter of my Father in Heaven, who loves me, and I love him."

The next day when the boy saw the pictures, he got quite a kick out of my creativity. I apologized for redecorating his room, and we parted friends. I didn't realize the impact my practical joke would have until later when the boy wrote me the following: "At first I took what you did in my room as a big joke. I even invited a bunch of kids from youth conference to come see your masterpieces. Everyone thought they were pretty funny. But then I started to really think about what you had written on those papers. It's true. Those girls are daughters of Heavenly Father, and I certainly haven't been looking at them that way. To see words about temple marriage on those kind of posters seemed so inconsistent. Suddenly it hit me that by having those pictures up on my walls I was being inconsistent, too. Needless to say, the posters came down."

Many attempt to rationalize poor choices by saying things like, "Everybody does it," "It's not that big a deal," "I can handle it," "It doesn't really affect me," "It's nothing I haven't seen before." Some even try to claim that the pornography they view is art. I remember taking an art history class at BYU in which we occasionally studied paintings or statues of nudes. When the instructor was asked if such pieces were pornographic, he explained the difference by defining two words: sensuous and sensual. He said nudity in art can be sensuous because its beauty appeals to the senses, while pornography is sensual because its only purpose is erotic arousal for commercial gain. The instructor's distinction has helped me a great deal in my own life as I draw the important lines between art and pornography, literature and lewdness.

When it comes to pornography, we must never open the door even the slightest crack, for as the ancient sage Rabbi Isaac once said of evil: "At first it is a wayfarer and a lodger. At last it becomes the master of the house" (Jon R. Haddon, "An Urge Toward Evil," *Reader's Digest,* November 1998, 48).

Watermark Visible in the Light

The new bill has a watermark that is clearly visible from both sides when held to the light. The security of those who struggle with pornography will likewise be more sure when they are willing to hold their actions to the light by seeking help. Those who have courage to admit their struggle to a bishop find a valuable friend and ally. In private interviews, some bishops will ask directly about pornography; others won't. Either way, it's up to those who struggle to bring their problem to light.

A commitment made to yourself can easily be broken. Commitments to God are often too easily postponed. But when commitments are made to another person, it puts on some pressure. It's pretty obvious that a person who arranges to exercise with a friend usually hangs in there longer than someone who does not. When the alarm goes off in the morning, it's easy to turn it off and roll over unless you know someone is waiting for you. Research studies have shown that those who make public commitments to quit smoking have a much greater chance of succeeding than those who try to do it secretly. Patients who make written commitments to take prescribed medicine are much more likely to follow through than patients who do not. When those who struggle with pornography know they will be seeing a bishop on Sunday morning, it may help them think twice about what they do on Saturday night.

However, as helpful as a spoken commitment can be, that is far from being the only reason to go to a bishop. As the father of the ward, he is authorized to receive revelation in your behalf. He can give you priesthood blessings and inspired counsel. He can help you formulate a positive plan of action and use priesthood keys to assist you in your quest to repent, draw closer to the Savior, and claim the wonderful blessings of Jesus Christ's atonement. You'll be amazed at the changes you can make when you stop relying on willpower alone and start relying on God's power.

Enlarged portraits, new backgrounds, microprinting, glowing thread, color shifting, and watermarks that are visible in the light: these are the security features that protect us from counterfeit money. They can also be reminders of what we need to do to detect and reject Satan's counterfeit of pornography.

Brad Wilcox grew up in Provo, Utah, except for childhood years spent in Ethiopia, Africa. He served a mission in Chile and is now married and has four children. He received a Ph.D. in education from the University of Wyoming in 1994. Brad was an associate professor in the Department of Teacher Education at Brigham Young University. He has served as the bishop of a BYU ward and recently returned from living with his family in New Zealand, where he directed a study abroad program. He now serves as a full-time mission president.

20

COMING HOME

Kathy Schlendorf

Coming home! What images will jump out of your memory
someday after you have left for college, for your mission, for
the first real job?

My first real homesickness was overwhelming. While I was living for a semester in Grenoble, France, every sight around me was
foreign. I concentrated so hard to understand the language, I had
constant headaches for the first few weeks. The humor was different, the writing on all the signs and stores was unreadable, hairdos
and clothing and cars and scenery were totally unfamiliar. I felt that
I had relocated on another planet.

The memories that I used to transport me to more familiar terri-
tory were similar to ones you have, I suspect. The fireplace with its
warmth and spitting logs; long evenings on the phone with my
friends; standing outside on the lawn with the hose and watching the
sun spill red paint across the clouds as it disappeared. Will you
remember autumn leaf fights after the piles of gold and brown and
yellow leaves have been raked? How about cutting down Christmas
trees in the snow? How about using the hot chocolate mug to thaw
your ice-sculpted fingers? And summer barbeques with corn on the
cob and cousins to laugh with? We used to slip away from the crowd
of family and go down to the stream and throw pebbles and wade
and splash.

Home.

For some of you, the memories of youth and family may bring back a different scene. Some of you have come to the gospel through very challenging doors. One summer, with others, I visited two neighboring stakes made up of both inner-city youth and of young people who lived in the more comfortable suburbs. As visitors, our first interest was to meet the youth and try to memorize their names. They were unbelievably patient with us as we barged up to them, interrupted their conversations, and introduced ourselves. As I was getting ready for my first attack, one of the stake youth leaders pointed out a husky black youth and told me his story. We'll call him Roderick.

This young man lives with his mother in one of the inner-city high-rise apartments. They have no car. No autumn leaves in a big yard to rake. Instead they live on poor streets with frustrated people who do not contribute to the ideal pumpkin carving, Christmas caroling, merit badge childhood.

Roderick and his mother found the gospel, but they live it in a very challenging environment. Even though their faithfulness does not insulate them from the realities of their lives, it does give them the courage and the tools to deal with the struggles they face. One day Roderick was waiting with his mother at the bus stop. Swaggering teens, clad in dirty jeans and matching bandannas, approached Roderick menacingly. He recognized the gang insignia and turned away. The gang leader shoved his shoulder. Roderick had no choice but to turn and face him.

"What gang do you belong to?" the cocky leader barked.

Roderick shook his head. "I don't belong to any gang."

The gang leader looked around at his friends and sneered. "Then you'd better join ours."

He shook his head again. Almost whispering, he said, "I don't want to belong to a gang." The leader took a pistol out of his pocket and shot Roderick in the gut at point-blank range.

His mother screamed, and the ink-clad boys scattered like cock-roaches vanishing into the woodwork. Her son was lying on the cement in his own blood.

There are many places where our earthly homes are not what they should be. In some homes there are harsh words that crack the surface of what could have been a place of trust and love. In some homes there is divorce. In others there is fear or poverty or sadness. One young woman asked a stake president what it was that she had done in the premortal life that was so horrible that her Heavenly Father had sent her to an abusive home, while other girls are sent to loving homes. The priesthood leader told her in a blessing that it was because of her valiancy; that she had volunteered to perform a Christlike service, to purify a lineage by absorbing the poison and not passing it on (see Carlfred Broderick, "The Uses of Adversity," in *As Women of Faith: Talks Selected from the BYU Women's Conferences,* ed. Mary E. Stovall and Carol Cornwall Madsen [Salt Lake City: Deseret Book Co., 1989], 177–78). We cannot judge why we are given the particular set of life experiences that is ours. Our choice is to become stronger because of them.

One fact I urge you to realize is this: we all came from a perfect heavenly home. Our Father and Mother were loving and strong and kind. There was no anger there; no one was ignored or spoiled; no one was overworked or left out. We were all friends.

When the announcement was made that it was time to come to earth, there was excitement at the chance to come here and to prove ourselves. Maybe it felt a little like tryouts. Those of you who make the team or the performing choir or the orchestra or the cheerleading squad know the rush of that success. Then comes the effort, the prac-tice, the sweat and concentration to succeed on the team. And earth life is like that. We have come here to make it possible to go home again—still as sons and daughters of God, to become like our Father and Mother in heaven.

My young black friend is a hero in my eyes. He may not drive a

Jeep or wear whatever brand is popular this season, but his soul is dressed in incredible finery because of the honor he wears. Wouldn't it be easier if, once the gang leader had taken out the gun and really tried this boy's courage, the cameraman could have yelled "Cut!" and the "actor" playing the bad guy could have laughed and slapped Roderick on the back and said, "Hey, man, this was only a test! You passed! Gimme five"?

Instead his mother got Roderick to a hospital, where the surgeon feared he would have to remove his intestines. After the operation, a surprised doctor told the mother that somehow the bullet had bypassed all the organs and simply cut through the muscle. He had never seen anything like it. We understand, don't we? Heavenly Father did not leave his faithful son alone. We may not be able to see him with our physical eyes, but he can see us with his. And he watches over us like the tender parent that he is. I believe that part of the nature of our earthly tests requires that we choose him (and we choose home) on faith.

Even though we must experience the bitter and the sweet experiences in life, won't that day come? Won't Heavenly Father welcome us one day and say, "Well done! You passed the test." And there will be tears. I miss that home every bit as much as I missed America while I was a student living in another country. Coming home. I want to be there.

Many years ago I met a young man who lived in the same farming community where I was living temporarily. I would often see him after supper working on his father's fields as I took one of the horses out for a quiet ride. He drove an old red tractor which was as much rust as it was paint. It rattled along loyally as he plowed, hauled hay, and went through the daily ritual of feeding his father's beavers. Every evening he would fell what seemed like a whole forest! He grabbed his ax and after two or three strokes each tree would fall to the ground. He would pile the trunks effortlessly in the wagon behind his tractor.

I was intrigued, so I followed him home. His mother was a gentle, quiet lady who baked bread and taught me to can fruit. She shared secrets about this youngest son which only contributed to the heroic image I already saw. He played sports; he played the piano. He had perfect attendance at Sunday School and seminary, and he quietly lived the gospel he knew.

That summer I watched him and his brothers add onto their modest farmhouse. His parents had raised five sons in three rooms, and in one effort they now doubled the size of their home. After all the construction was complete, the family realized that there was no money left to carpet the new wing. My young friend made a private trip to the bank and withdrew one thousand dollars from his savings account—money he had earned by hauling hay all the previous summer. Secretly he sneaked the money to his mother. She had her new carpet.

This boy grew up and all the qualities I saw just got better. He completed a year of college before his mission, and returned older and wiser from two years of service to the Lord. I had the script for the rest of his life all written out: Temple marriage. A youth leader. A Little League coach for his own sons. A life of quiet, faithful service to match the twenty-one years he had already lived.

Time did pass, but the script changed. I never knew what triggered it—he wouldn't tell me—but he made choices that took him on a detour. A friend died tragically in a boating accident. Did he doubt what he knew about eternal life? His father's hidden abusiveness surfaced again. Did he wonder how Heavenly Father could allow bad things to happen through people who should know better? Did the lure of temptation simply sound more tantalizing than the promises of the gospel? That seemed impossible, knowing what I knew of him. All I do know is that he chose a counterfeit. He closed the door on Heavenly Father and on all of us. This pearl of a youth—this hero that everyone loved—locked his heart away and was gone. I pounded on the wall he had built, but it was as if he was too far away to hear.

As the years passed, he never returned. Nothing I could say seemed to matter to him at all, but instead of letting him go, I refused to write him off. He was my friend, and if he didn't come back, home would be lonely.

He became a dairyman, married, and had two sons. Because he left the Church did he become hardened and bitter and sinful? No. He was still the gentle, smiling friend he had always been. There was a wall, and he kept us at a distance, but he stayed the man I had always admired, working as hard as ever; only this time it was in the middle of the black morning hours, milking a herd of cows. I don't understand much about the economy, but I know that farmers depend on stable prices to make ends meet. I never could get the details into my head, but one year his farm failed, and he lost everything.

For a time he became a truck driver. He had a huge rig and drove it to all the corners of the United States. He was on the road for days and then only home for a weekend or so before leaving again. He began to hate what he was doing. Occasionally, when school was out, he would take one of his sons with him. Those boys loved the high seat, the huge wheels, and the bed in back. They constantly rummaged through the small fridge and ate whenever they wanted to. The boys felt as if they were on a giant moving playground. For my friend it was not as much fun.

During this time he stopped at our home when his route took him our way, and we would sit over a meal and visit. One of these times he became very reflective, and he said to me with tears behind his eyes: "Kathy, I have come to realize how much family means to me. I don't ever want to do anything that would make it so I couldn't go home again." His boys didn't have their dad every day, and his wife had to be both the mom and the dad. He felt so hopeless being separated from them.

I stared at him. Don't you hear what you're saying? What about our heavenly home? What will it be like one day if you are not there and the loneliness I feel for you now becomes eternal?

We all have challenges in this life (even the people who live on the hill and seem to have it so easy and so comfortable). Heavenly Father has tailored each life's lesson in our own privately constructed classrooms. Trust your Heavenly Father. He knows what you are going through, and he is there. Just keep your focus on the fact that this life is a test. And every day, choose him. Choose home.

I recognize (from experience) that this sounds a lot easier than it is to do. As we get tumbled around in life's whirlpool, sometimes we grumble: "If I really had a Father in Heaven, he wouldn't let this happen to me." "Is this another fairy tale like Santa Claus and the Easter bunny?" "Are Mom and Dad using this heaven and hell thing as a way to get me to do what they think is right?" When we buy into these lines, we open doors that take us out of the protection of the gospel net.

My cute son was thirteen the summer he discovered gasoline. He dipped used tennis balls into gasoline and then set them on fire and used a baseball bat to hit them. I was not home, of course, and it was great fun. By some miracle he did not kill himself or his friends, and I suppose you didn't either when you went through that phase.

One weekend when I was gone to a youth conference, he and a friend thought it would be fun to draw gasoline designs in the backyard grass and then set them on fire. He wondered what it would look like. So the boys ignited their design with a match, and the fire hissed through the yard, burning the lush, thick green grass that I had spent tons of money and effort on. The design burned furiously, and my son saw that he would soon burn up the entire yard. He turned on the sprinklers in a panic and doused the flames. The next day I came home.

With sincere remorse in his eyes (and we moms can read eyes), I recognized that he meant what he told me. "Mom, I am really sorry. I honestly didn't realize it would kill the grass." He thought it would burn the gas but not the grass. I guess it didn't kill the cement when he had done something similar on the cement. "I won't ever do that again!" he promised. And I knew he meant, "Please don't kill me."

I think sometimes we do things because we really don't understand the consequences. We can hear it over and over, but curiosity still wins out, and we experiment. Then we have to choose again. "Okay, I blew it. I can either admit that I made a mistake and ask for forgiveness, or I can stubbornly hold on to my mistake and convince myself that it is not a mistake. If there is no God, then there is no sin, therefore I cannot be wrong." Instead of stopping and turning around, we set the grass on fire over and over until there is no grass left. Along the way we decide that God is a fairy tale used by parents and leaders to scare us into complying with unreasonable rules. Which choice makes the most sense?

As I sensed his genuine remorse, my job was to forgive. I gulped back my first reaction (you can guess what that was) and hugged him and teased him. The grass grew back. Do you think your Heavenly Father is less loving and forgiving and understanding than your parents? He is the perfect example of the qualities we try to copy. He sent his Son to make up for the moments of weakness we fall into. He expected us to make mistakes, but he wants us to recognize that is what we are doing and change the negative patterns before they get set in concrete.

Once, many years ago, I was caught in the trap I have described. I felt that I just couldn't live the way celestial people lived (I had some image that other members of the Church were perfect—and then there was me). I decided I wasn't good enough, and since that was true, I might as well "enjoy myself." That usually means we want to sin and are trying to figure out a way to justify it.

I had decided to leave the Church. I remember the morning after making this decision. I was combing my hair in the bathroom mirror.

A face seemed to be looking back at me that wasn't my face. It was a kind, gentle, dark-haired man's face, and he had a soft short beard and incredibly sad eyes. He looked at me, and inside my mind I heard him ask, "Are you leaving me, Kathy?" I looked away because in my mind I knew that he knew, and I couldn't look at him. The face followed me. "Where are you going?" he asked again. I lowered my eyes and said aloud, "Nowhere." There is nowhere else. The path is set. I can walk on it, or I can leave it. I get to choose.

"Jesus saith unto him, I am the way, the truth, and the life: no man cometh unto the Father, but by me" (John 14:6). I needed to retake my spiritual pulse. I had allowed dozens of little things to combine into a huge web that blinded me. Because of the atonement of the Savior, there are no sins common to man which cannot be fixed. It may take time; it may require a lot of humility and effort, but the grass will grow back.

A Lamanite king heard the gospel and wanted desperately to know if it was true. He asked, "What shall I do that I may have this eternal life of which thou hast spoken? Yea, what shall I do that I may be born of God, having this wicked spirit rooted out of my breast, and receive his Spirit, that I may be filled with joy, that I may not be cast off at the last day?" He too wanted to come home after earth life was over. "I will forsake my kingdom, that I may receive this great joy" (Alma 22:15). Aaron explained how the king could obtain a testimony of the gospel. All he had to do was to ask in faith, and to repent of his sins. That is what we all have to do. "The king did bow down before the Lord, upon his knees . . . and cried mightily, saying: O God, Aaron hath told me that there is a God; and if there is a God, and if thou art God, wilt thou make thyself known unto me, and I will give away all my sins to know thee" (Alma 22:17–18).

The world holds out a smorgasbord of sins. They look delicious. They seem tantalizing. We are pulled like metal shavings to the magnet unless we decide to walk past the table. Trials can defeat us if we let them. Pain and hurt can defeat us if we let it wedge in between us and our faith in our Heavenly Father. Joseph Smith really did have a vision in a quiet grove of trees. It changed his life, and it has changed ours. The Church is true. That is no longer the question. The question now is can we be true?

Coming home. Be there.

Kathy Schlendorf joined the Church when she was fifteen years old. She teaches English and French at a middle school in Provo, Utah, and taught early morning seminary for eight years. Kathryn studied for a year in France and traveled the world with a Brigham Young University group in 1966. She has taught at EFY and in other programs since 1983.

21

"THE SPIRIT SPEAKETH THE TRUTH AND LIETH NOT"

John Bytheway

A s a young man or young woman, you may not remember it, but late 1989 was an amazing time. The nightly news was dominated by the story of the breakup of the Soviet Union. For years, the prophets had asked us to pray that the nations of the earth would open their doors to the missionaries, and it began to happen before our eyes. The "Iron Curtain" as it used to be called, was drawn open, and the "Cold War" was over. Also, the Berlin Wall came down. If I understand my history correctly, following World War II, the Communists kept half of the German city of Berlin, and eventually built a wall around it—27 miles of concrete and barbed wire—completely dividing East Berlin from West Berlin. Families and friends were separated for decades. But on November 9, 1989, the wall came down. The TV news captured scenes of tearful reunions and joyous celebrations. They also showed happy people using sledgehammers to smash the wall that had separated them for so long from the rest of the world. With this bit of history in mind, you can imagine my gratitude when a friend who had been traveling in Europe, presented me with a small chunk of the Berlin wall. It's not beautiful to look at. Its edges are not smooth and polished. You wouldn't call it colorful; it's mostly gray and black except on the flat side, where it's been sprayed with purple and red paint. It's not expensive, as some precious stones are, but it's very precious to me. Sometimes when I look at this little piece of history I think about all those who are now able to enjoy the blessings of freedom because the wall came down. Many East German people over the years tried to get beyond the wall. Some were successful, others were killed. Now the blessings of freedom are available to all because the wall came down.

Sometimes, without realizing what we're doing, we build walls around ourselves. We want the blessings of the gospel, but if we're not careful we shut out the Spirit of the Lord by putting up walls. Our Heavenly Father earnestly wants to get through to us, but he will not force his way in. We must bring down the walls and let him in. Elder H. Burke Peterson wrote: "As we go through life, we oft-times build a rock wall between ourselves and heaven. This wall is built by our unrepented sins. . . . In spite of the wall we build in front of us, when we cry out to the Lord, he still sends his messages from heaven; but instead of being able to penetrate our hearts, they hit the wall that we have built up and bounce off. His messages don't penetrate, so we say, 'He doesn't hear,' or 'He doesn't answer.' Sometimes this wall is very formidable, and the great challenge of life is to destroy it, or, if you please, to cleanse ourselves, purifying this inner vessel so that we can be in tune with the Spirit" (*Ensign,* June 1981, 73).

If we will bring down the walls, we will be better able to receive answers to our prayers and guidance for solving our problems. The Spirit will teach us things that are not otherwise obtainable. The Spirit is a *teacher.*

The fifteen-year-old young lady who wrote the following letter was taught by the Spirit. She wrote this letter during a presentation at a youth conference. The Spirit was there to teach her, and she listened to what it said. Read carefully her words:

"I'm writing you 'cause I need to talk, okay? Lately I've had a lot of problems with morality and the Word of Wisdom and my friends and family. I want to change so bad but I honestly don't know how. Yeah, I'll be fine right now while I'm here surrounded by the youth, but I'm afraid to go home to my friends. I'll change now, but when I go back I'm going back to my drinking friends and my foul-mouth friends, etc.

"I can stand strong with the youth behind me, but alone I'm afraid. I'm afraid I will give in. I'm afraid of what my friends might say, or will they laugh? My (kinda) boyfriend I don't want to go back to. I don't want him to touch me or come near me or talk to me or anything! I want a guy to like me for me and not for any other reason. One that is my friend as well as my boyfriend."(The word *kinda* was written in later, scrunched between the other two words.)

Sometime between the beginning and the end of the conference, the boy she was dating changed in status from her "boyfriend" to her "kinda boyfriend," whom she didn't want to see or associate with ever again. Why? Did the speaker point at her from the pulpit and command her to change her boyfriend? No. The speaker wasn't even talking about dating or the law of chastity! What really happened? She was in a meeting where the Spirit was present. The *Spirit* spoke softly to her heart and told her that she needed to change her situation. Fortunately, she put herself in a position to feel the Spirit (she attended the conference), and then she listened to what it was telling her deep inside—things about her life that no one else knew.

Not only will the Spirit speak to our hearts and tell us what is amiss in our lives, but it will also give us the courage and strength to follow through. Many of the things we may learn from the Spirit may be hard for us to put into our lives.

Following is a letter from a young lady who attended Especially for Youth: "Thank you so much for the session of Especially for Youth. It was one of the most inspiring weeks of my life. I hope it will not fade away. Thanks again for your work."

Big deal, right? Would you like to hear the rest of the story? This letter comes from the mother of the young lady: "How can we thank you for what you have done for our daughter? She called us when

EFY was over and was ecstatic over her experience. She said her testimony had been strengthened greatly, and that many of her prayers were answered. She took avid notes during the talks, and was grateful for the copies of the other presentations also. . . . This summer is a crucial time for our daughter, as a less-active boy with several good qualities, but not the right ones, is determined to keep her out of circulation until he can someday marry her. EFY, it appears, has given her the strength to break things off. Our cup runneth over with gratitude!"

I'd like to rewrite that last sentence to say: "The *Spirit,* it appears, has given her the strength to break things off." The Spirit will give you the power to change your life.

I'm sure that if you think back you can remember times when you've been taught by the Spirit. You've felt that you wanted to be a better person. Not better looking or more popular, just better. That's what happens when you bring down the walls and allow the Spirit of the Lord to enter. The Spirit reminds us of and pulls us toward our God-given potential.

Sometime in the future you'll have those feelings again. Perhaps while you're reading this book. Perhaps at a family home evening, or during a Church meeting or seminary class. Maybe during your own scripture study. When that happens, take some time and look deep into the feelings of your heart. Ask yourself some questions. What would the Lord have me do? You might ask: "Should I marry in the temple?" "Am I dating the type of person who would take me there?" You might ask: "Should I serve a mission?" "Am I keeping myself clean so that I may go?" What has the Spirit told you? "For the Spirit speaketh the truth and lieth not. Wherefore, it speaketh of things as they really are, and of things as they really will be; wherefore, these things are manifested unto us plainly, for the salvation of our souls" (Jacob 4:13).

What wonderful words: "The Spirit speaketh the truth and lieth not." That is why it is so important that we *hear* what it says, and then *do* what we've heard. The Spirit is sent from God, who loves us perfectly and wants our success, so we must hear and do. "Ye are commanded in all things to ask of God, who giveth liberally; and *that which the Spirit testifies unto you even so I would that ye should do* in all holiness of heart, walking uprightly before me, considering the end of your salvation, doing all things with prayer and thanksgiving" (D&C 46:7; emphasis added).

This chapter is not intended to tell you all the ways that we can sin or build walls against the Spirit—no chapter could do that. It is written in the hope that you will open your heart to the will of the Lord for your life, even if that heart has been closed for a long time. Sometimes things happen to us in our lives or in our families that make it hard for us to believe in anything anymore. The Lord does not want us to remain in darkness. He wants to help us understand. But we must bring down the walls and invite him in.

Many scriptures offer this metaphor: Seek, and ye shall find; ask, and ye shall receive; knock, and it shall be opened. There is one scripture, however, in which Jesus is on the other side of the door. *He* is the one who is patiently knocking, hoping that we will invite him in. "Behold, I stand at the door, and knock: if any man hear my voice, and open the door, I will come in to him, and will sup with him, and he with me" (Revelation 3:20).

Because of the gift of agency (which in the premortal life we fought valiantly to keep), each one of us has a door into his life and into his heart. We can choose whom to let in and whom to keep out. Satan wanted to rob us of our agency (Moses 4:3). The Savior, on the other hand, will not force us back to heaven. He won't even force open the door. Patiently, persistently, he stands at your door and knocks. While you are at school, fighting the daily battle for self-esteem and acceptance, where people are mercilessly teased because they're overweight or different or "dumb," he is there knocking. When you feel alone and afraid and that nobody cares, he is there. Still. Knocking at your door. Please let him in.

How sad it must make Father in Heaven to see some who willingly open other doors into their hearts while shutting the Savior out! How sad that people who fought so valiantly to keep their agency in the premortal life now seem almost eager to give it away by getting themselves addicted to drugs, alcohol, or pornography! If they could only remember who they are! Some of the other doors lead to an escape in the world, whereas the Savior offers an escape *from* the world. He will still knock. Softly, patiently, persistently, he will knock. Please let him in.

Some of us feel that we can't do anything, that we haven't any great talents to offer. We see others with their good looks, their talents or social skills, and it makes it hard for us to like ourselves. Again, the answer to these feelings lies in opening the door to the Lord. Where does self-esteem really come from? Read carefully these words by Elder James E. Faust: "I testify that as we mature spiritually under the guidance of the Holy Ghost, *our sense of personal worth, of belonging, and of identity increases.* I further testify that *I would rather have every person enjoy the Spirit of the Holy Ghost than any other association,* for they will be led by the Spirit to light and truth and pure intelligence, which can carry them back into the presence of God" ("The Gift of the Holy Ghost—A Sure Compass," *Ensign,* May 1989, 33; emphasis added).

If I had a wish for every young person who might read this book it would be that they would make their own spiritual well-being their first priority; that they would pray each day to learn and grow in a better way than they have ever done before; that they would love God with all their heart, as he has loved them. I have met young people who are like this. I love them, and I admire them. They are heroes to me.

Here's an excerpt of a letter from Rodney: "I was coming home from a football game, and the group I was riding with, about five guys, knew I didn't drink or smoke because of my religion. Well, they promised that they wouldn't drink on the way up or back, so I told them: 'Thanks, I don't care what you do after, just as long as I get home safe' (joking with them). Well on the way home they pulled out some beer, saying they couldn't resist any longer. I was stunned! They started to pass a can of beer around, taking sips or drinks. When it got to me I just calmly threw it out the window. They were shocked, but then they all decided that they didn't need it and threw the rest out the window. I knew I had done what was right."

I understand why such young people are called a chosen generation. For them, obedience is a quest and not an irritation. They don't say, "I can't drink," "I can't see vulgar movies," and so forth. They say, "I don't want to drink," "I don't want to see vulgar movies." In effect they say, "I don't want to do anything that might build a wall between me and the Lord."

President Gordon B. Hinckley has said: "You are part of a marvelous generation, the best in the history of this Church. You read all about drugs and youth going down the road that leads to destruction. There are millions of them in this land. But I want to say that I believe with all my heart we have the finest generation of youth in this Church that we have ever had. I believe that. They know the gospel better. They know the scriptures a lot better than some of us. They are bright, energetic, faithful, clean, virtuous, and they have ambition. God bless you, my beloved young friends. I do love you. I want you to know that. I pray for you. I pray constantly that I can do something to help the young people of this Church move along to greater accomplishment while keeping the faith and being true to the traditions of their forebears" (*Teachings of Gordon B. Hinckley* [Salt Lake City: Deseret Book Co., 1997], 720).

You are choice spirits. You have been sent to this world in a very difficult time. Every day, in temples throughout the world, prayers are offered for the youth of the Church. There will be difficult decisions for you to make in the years to come—decisions about missions, marriage, schooling, and career. Help is available. Please let the Lord help you. It is my prayer that you will immerse yourselves in the scriptures and pray fervently to your Father in Heaven, who loves you not only for what you are, but for what you may become.

Bring down the walls and open the door. Learn to receive answers from the Spirit, which "speaketh the truth and lieth not" (Jacob 4:13).

John Bytheway is from Salt Lake City, Utah. He served his mission in the Philippines, and later graduated from Brigham Young University. He is currently finishing up his master's degree in religious education at BYU, and working as an administrator at Deseret Book Company. John and his wife, Kimberly, have three children.

22

ALWAYS REMEMBER

Scott Anderson

It was a small class, and I was one of only sixteen students. The cost of tuition had pressed my meager budget to the limit, so, to get my money's worth, I was trying to learn all I could. One day at the end of class, the teacher announced, "Next time we meet, we will be playing show-and-tell, so bring something that is meaningful to you to share with the class."

What? We are going to play show-and-tell in my college class? That's a kindergarten game!

As I left campus and headed to work, I thought, *Why am I wasting my time in this class?* But, then, I began to think about the possibilities. Many members of my class were not members of the Church, and I had just been home from my mission for a short while. Maybe I could share my flipchart with them and briefly review all six discussions! Then again, maybe not. But, what if I shared the 1870 edition of the old German Bible that I had been given by a family that I had baptized on my mission?

With Bible in hand, I slipped into class two days later, prepared to share a glimpse into my mission. What followed was an experience I would never forget. Students shared things such as photos, grass skirts from Hawaii (that is a story for another day!), and one student even brought a football. About forty minutes after class had begun, a fellow classmate came into the room. She listened as two of the others showed their treasures and described their significance. When they were finished, the teacher called on the young lady and asked if she had forgotten the assignment. She assured him that she had not forgotten but that she had been walking around campus for the previous forty minutes trying to decide if she had the courage to share with us what mattered most to her.

Then she reverently held up a small gold ring. I still remember the sympathy I felt for her as she fought back the tears and shared her story:

"I was three years old at the time. My mother came to tuck me into bed and stayed for a long time. She cried and told me she loved me, then said as she tied this ring around my little wrist, 'No matter what happens, always look at this ring and remember that there is a mother in the world who loves you very much!'

"When I woke up the next morning, she was gone. It was some time before my grandmother came by and helped me pack my things. Within a week, I was in an orphanage and was experiencing challenges that I had never known of before. I was lonely and afraid. I had many questions and a constant feeling that my mother would return, but I didn't know when. Morning after morning, I awoke alone—lost and confused. This went on for months, until one day I was taken from the crowded commons room and escorted into the office.

"An American couple who were in Germany serving in the military were waiting to meet me. They spoke very little German, and it was difficult to understand what was happening. However, before many hours had passed, I was riding with them in their car and had been told they were to be my new parents. I was frightened and cried and cried. As it turned out, they were the kindest, most wonderful people that any child could hope to have as parents.

"All the time I was growing up, my ring remained a constant reminder that somewhere in the world I had another mother who loved me. I felt compelled to return someday to try to find her. That desire became a driving force in my life. During high school, I didn't participate in other activities because I was working to save the money to go to Europe to search for my other family. After many years of constant effort, as a graduation trip, I traveled to Europe. I had researched carefully and knew the town and directions to my family homestead. So, I left my tour group at the location nearest to my birthplace and traveled on a local bus for a few hours.

"I arrived at the city and after a long walk, I climbed the hill and found the home where I had lived as a little girl. There was smoke curling up from the chimney. I realized that the home was still registered to my family's name—that in this house was the link to my roots. I sat on the hillside for hours watching the home and thinking. This moment was what I had dreamt of for years. Then, without approaching the home, I turned and walked away, never knocking on the door."

She continued, "This little ring has been a constant reminder in my life, not only that I have a birth mother who loves me, but of so much more." Then, with great feeling, this courageous young lady said, "When I look at this ring I am grateful for all the sacrifice it represents. You see, if my mother hadn't left me to be adopted, I might never have found The Church of Jesus Christ of Latter-day Saints. I love being a Mormon more than any other thing in my life. That is what I think about when I see this ring!"

I found out in that classroom that grown-up show-and-tell is quite a different thing than it was in kindergarten. I have never forgotten the emotional presentation given by my classmate and have often thought of how her ring was a way for her to remember her mother's love for her and her gratitude for the power of the Lord in her life.

We are lucky if we have in our lives a few symbols of the things we treasure most. I am grateful that our Heavenly Father has given us a pair of symbols to remind us of his love for us and the gift he has given us of his Son, Jesus Christ. We partake of these symbols each week as we participate in the sacrament and are given the opportunity to remember.

When the Savior first blessed and administered the sacrament to his beloved disciples, I can only imagine his thoughts and feelings. He knew he was about to leave them and that they would face great challenges in his absence. How could he help them remember him in their greatest times of need? How could he ensure that his Spirit would always be with them?

As the Passover feast was coming to a close, the Savior took bread and blessed and broke it. He gave it to his disciples, saying, "Take, eat; this is my body. And he took the cup, and gave thanks, and gave it to them, saying, Drink ye all of it; For this is my blood of the new testament, which is shed for many for the remission of sins" (Matthew 26:26–28). What greater constant reminder could there be than bread, the staff of life, and water, the most common liquid on earth? These two sustain our lives and so are appropriate reminders of the Savior's role as the Bread of Life and the Living Water.

In 3 Nephi in the Book of Mormon, we are told that the Savior administered the sacrament twice to help the people always remember. Can you imagine the thoughts that went through the minds of our Nephite brothers and sisters as they partook of the sacrament after he was gone? They had had the sacred privilege of thrusting their hands into his side and reverently touching the prints of the nails in his hands and feet. He had also manifested his great love for them by healing their sick and blessing their children. They had the physical evidence of his reality and resurrection and had partaken directly of his love. How can we, who were not present to feel the prints of the nails in his hands, remember him always?

Elder Dallin H. Oaks gives us a key to remembering our Savior. He states: "To remember means to keep in memory. In the scriptures, it often means to keep a person in memory, together with associated emotions like love, loyalty, or gratitude. The stronger the emotion, the more vivid and influential the memory."

Elder Oaks gives three examples:

1. "Most of us have the clearest memories of our mortal parents, who gave us birth and nurtured us through childhood. This kind of memory does not dim with the passing years, but with wisdom and perspective becomes ever more meaningful. As I grow older, I think more frequently of my father and my mother. I will always remember them.

2. "Shortly before my wife was to give birth to our first child, we learned that the baby must be born by cesarean section. I was then a student at Brigham Young University, going to school full time and working almost full time. From my meager earnings, a little over $1.00 an hour, we had saved enough money for the hospital and doctor bills, but nothing in our plans or emotions had prepared us for this shocking announcement. We scarcely knew what a cesarean birth was, and we feared the worst.

"A few days later we faced our ordeal. After what seemed an eternity, I stood at a window in the hospital hallway, looking into a basket containing our firstborn. The joy of seeing her and knowing that my beloved companion had survived the operation was inexpressible. As I experienced that moment, I became aware of a stranger standing beside me. He introduced himself as Dr. N. Frederick Hicken, the surgeon who had come from Salt Lake City to perform the operation. His presence reminded me that a surgeon's fee had not been in our plans, and I began to ask him if I could pay his fee over a period of time. 'Don't worry about that, young man,' he said in a kindly way. 'This is one from the Hickens to the Oakses.' Before I could stammer a thank-you, he was gone.

"I was filled with wonder at this unexpected gift. Our benefactor must have known my father, a young medical doctor who died when I was a boy. He must have given us this gift because of something my father had done. I marveled at the goodness of this man who had come to us in our crisis and had, without recompense, used his powers to preserve the lives of those I loved. The emotion of that moment made the memory indelible. The name of that doctor is precious to me. I will always remember him.

3. "Some time ago, someone praised me for something I had done. Even as I received that compliment I knew I did not deserve it. The credit belonged to wise and wonderful teachers who had taught me what to do and how to do it. My teachers were memorable. I shudder to think what I would have lost if teachers had not helped me want to learn and then taught me what I needed to know. I will always be grateful to my teachers. I will always remember them.

"By now you must surely realize that I have given these three examples because the reasons why I will always remember these persons are related to the reasons why we should always remember Jesus Christ: He is our Creator, our Redeemer, and our Teacher" ("Always Remember Him," *Ensign,* May 1988, 29–30).

One Sunday during the presentation of the sacrament, our children (who were quite young at the time) made a little disturbance, and I realized that I hadn't shared with them sufficient understanding of why we remember the Savior in this important way. I also had a prompting of what I needed to do to help them.

The next night our wonderful neighbors agreed to spend family home evening with us. We shared a brief video presentation about the Savior's life and then headed for the cemetery in our little town. As we quietly gathered around a little graveside, a spirit of reverence settled on our group. Sweet Sister Dunn began to share her memories of her daughter Emily.

She told us that during her three-year-old birthday party, Emily became quite sick. Brother and Sister Dunn took their young daughter to the doctor and were sent home with some pain medication for her to take. However, she became even more sick during the night, and they ended up taking her this time to the hospital emergency room. It was discovered that her appendix had ruptured and that the infection was running throughout her body. Only those who have watched a loved one suffer can imagine the struggle they went through.

At about 2:00 A.M., while standing outside the intensive care unit, Sister Dunn pleaded with Heavenly Father for her little one's life. She heard a quiet question: "Do you have enough faith to ask for Emily to live?" As she searched her deepest feelings, she knew that she could answer, "Yes, yes, I do!"

Then came the second question: "Do you have enough faith to let her go?" Hours later she was still struggling within to find the strength to honestly answer. Finally, after many hours, peace filled her heart, and she was able to answer, "Yes, I do." Moments later the doctor informed her that Emily had passed away.

Bishop Dunn had been quietly standing next to his wife in the cemetery. As she finished her beautiful testimony of faith and peace, he began to share his feelings. Following Emily's passing, he had not had a peaceful experience at first. He had felt lonely and empty. He described the way Emily would greet him at the front door with some new, exciting discovery as he arrived home from work each day. Then she would wrap her little hand around his thumb and drag him out into the yard to find a new flower or a beautiful plant. He said that after she died, he didn't even want to go in the front door. It was just too hard.

Then, about a month after her death, he had a dream. In his dream he was in a crowded room. He heard Emily's voice, and she came to him, wrapped her hand around his thumb, and invited him to follow her. They made their way through the crowd and came to a door. She opened it and pulled him through it into a room. As the door closed behind them, Emily let go of her father's thumb and in a few short steps was enfolded in the loving arms of the Savior. Bishop Dunn said that he awoke on a pillow that was wet with tears, and as he shared that sacred experience with us—of seeing his Emily at peace, cradled in the Savior's arms—he testified that he also felt the Savior's love and finally found the peace that had eluded him.

It was a moving and beautiful experience that day in the cemetery. The Spirit of the Lord was present, and our children felt it. It was a perfect time to explain to them that every week we are invited to attend another sacred memorial service, one where another Father wants to share with us insights and information about the life and death of his Beloved Son. We discussed the importance of listening to what the Lord has to say to us during sacrament time. And we pointed out how much we would miss if we were to talk or not pay attention.

We all agreed that we would try very hard during the sacrament to understand what our Heavenly Father would like to teach us and to think harder about what it means to renew our sacred covenants with him.

The next week as we were singing the sacrament hymn, I whispered to the children a reminder of our experience in the cemetery. It made a difference—not only for them, but for me.

Each of you has had some kind of experience in which you have felt the Spirit. Perhaps that tender feeling has come to you during EFY, seminary, family home evening, Young Men or Young Women meetings, sacrament meeting, Sunday School, or while reading the scriptures (feasting on the word), praying, doing service, preparing for a mission and temple marriage, or attending the temple. As we recall such experiences, they give us courage and faith to do our part. What is our part? Our part is to be willing to take his name upon us, keep his commandments, and always remember him (see Moroni 4:3). As Elder Oaks said, we want to remember all that he has *created* for us, that he is our *redeemer,* and that he will be our *teacher* if we will allow him to be.

We can reap the rewards of the great show-and-tell scriptural promise: "The words of Christ will *tell* you all things what ye should do. . . . if ye will enter in by the way, and receive the Holy Ghost, it will *show* unto you all things what ye should do" (2 Nephi 32:3, 5;

emphasis added). We can then know that as we do our part, the Savior will take us home with him to our Heavenly Father.

That is my prayer for each of you.

Scott Anderson served a mission to South Germany, and then married Angelle Clark in the Salt Lake Temple. They are the parents of seven children and grandparents of eleven—nine of them boys. Brother Anderson has a Ph.D. in Marriage and Family Therapy from BYU. He has taught for thirty years in the Church Education System, and is a faculty member at the Orem Institute of Religion adjacent to Utah Valey State College. Brother Anderson enjoys home construction projects, writing, running, and making memories with his family. He loves to teach and share his love of the Savior and His gospel. He has been involved in the "Especially for Youth" Program since it began. He and his wife have enjoyed serving as missionary companions in their ward in Bluffdale, Utah.

INDEX